SOMETHING PAINFUL THIS WAY COMES

by

Timothy James

*I would like to dedicate this book to my dearest and best friend,
Jennifer.*

*As a young woman, wide-eyed with optimism, you said you would
stay with me for richer or for poorer,
in sickness and in health.*

*You had no idea how much those words would be tested, but you
have stayed true to them for over 25 years.*

*I am so thankful that we have been able to go on this journey
together.*

You are the greatest gift God has ever given me.

TABLE OF CONTENTS

WHISPERS, GROANS AND PRAYERS

ACKNOWLEDGEMENTS

INTRODUCTION

It is 2012 and I am in the midst of a season of suffering.

I don't know exactly where in this season I am. I hope that I am nearing the end, as it has been going on for about a year and a half now; I had hoped I was nearing the end a year ago. I may be in the middle of a three-year season of suffering, or maybe I am still in the early stages of a ten-year season of suffering. All I know for sure is that I am somewhere in the midst of it now.

In writing this book, I considered describing my ordeal in detail so as to justify my use of the term "suffering", but I quickly realized that would be a pointless venture. Sure, some would read it and think, "Oh my goodness, he really is suffering" because what I am going through is worse than anything they have experienced. However, others might read it and think, "You call that suffering?" Their personal stories would make my struggle look like a walk in the park.

I came to realize that it is meaningless to compare one person's experiences of suffering with another's. When you go to see the doctor, she will ask you how bad your experience of pain is on a scale of one to ten. If you say it is a two, she will believe that it is a two. If you say it is a ten, she will believe it is a ten (and probably give you something to help adjust your perception of the pain towards the aforementioned two). There is no objective scale with which to measure pain. In the same way, there is no objective scale with which to measure suffering.

I once met a woman dying of AIDS in a Mother Teresa hospital in Mumbai, India. She was a beautiful woman with a warm, sweet smile. The room in which she lived was simple; four concrete walls enclosed the tiny space with one window and one door. She shared the room with three other women, just like her, who were dying of AIDS. She asked me to play my guitar while she sang me a song. I did my best to try and match my western musical understanding to her eastern melody. However, I quickly discovered that musical perfection did not really matter. What mattered was how joyfully she sang her song. I was astounded at how someone enduring terminal suffering in a place of such poverty could be filled with so much joy. I wonder how she would rate her level of suffering.

I am continually amazed at the level of suffering humans can actually endure. If you search "People are Awesome" on YouTube, you will see what I mean. There are quite a few videos tagged with this phrase, which portray men and women carrying out seemingly impossible feats. Often these feats involve a significant amount of danger. I know from my paltry attempts at thrilling endeavors (like trampolining or unicycling) that success doesn't come without pain. The guy on roller blades dropping from a dizzying height to a ramp below him, did not get to that level of skill without numerous bumps, bruises and broken bones.

Athletes at every level of sport are willing to subject their bodies to all kinds of suffering, hoping to push beyond their known limits.

In the business world, many leaders are willing to work long hours, sacrificing personal health and relationships; in fact they choose to repeat this pattern for years on end.

I met another beautiful person at that Mother Teresa hospital in Mumbai. She was a little girl, poorest of the poor, who had been abandoned to die by her family. She had no legs and only one arm. The Sisters of Charity cared for her daily needs. She lay crying in her crib, but when she saw me, her face lit up and she waved at me. I went over and picked her up. She wrapped her one arm around me and giggled continuously as she kissed my cheek. It was all I could do to keep from weeping as I saw the amount of suffering this poor daughter of God had to endure. And yet, she did endure.

I had the privilege of visiting Manshiyat Naser, also known as Garbage City, a slum settlement on the outskirts of Cairo, Egypt. Although the area has streets, shops, and apartments - as do other areas of the city, it lacks infrastructure and often has no running water, sewage, or electricity. All the garbage of Cairo is delivered to Garbage City, where it is meticulously picked over by hand to retrieve any potentially useful or recyclable items. I made my way slowly through the slum, passing massive storerooms filled with immense piles of garbage. Whole families were working together to painstakingly sort through the refuse. I don't need to describe the odor and filth that I saw. And yet, I was often greeted with bright smiles and waving hands. I could hear laughter and joking in some of the rooms. Sure, there were many who held the look of despair, but even they continued on. I was humbled as I saw the depths of suffering they were able to endure.

This amazes me.

Several times in my own journey, I have come to the place where I thought I couldn't go on; the suffering was simply too much to endure. And then, astonishingly, I did go on. In fact, I seem to have an unbreakable desire to go on, to endure even more pain.

One of my favorite lines from the 1987 movie "The Princess Bride" is delivered by the Dread Pirate Roberts in response to Princess Buttercup's query of suffering. He says,

"Life is pain, Highness, anyone who tells you different is selling you something."

Life is pain. There is no avoiding it. Here in the west we have taken great strides to try and minimize that pain; in some ways, we have been successful. But there is still a truckload of pain that we can't seem to avoid. The reality is that each one of us suffers: divorce, poverty, broken relationships, sickness, failure, disgrace, shame, fear, depression, loneliness, bullying, loss, death.

But while everyone experiences suffering, not everyone handles it in the same way. There are terrible responses to suffering and there are positive ways to handle suffering. I have found that my response to suffering has been directly related to my understanding of God's role in the midst of my suffering.

I'm going to approach the subject of suffering from my perspective as a believer in, and follower of, Jesus Christ. In my view, the way a religion addresses suffering might just be one of the most important foundations of that spiritual system, and I have found the teachings of Jesus to be exceptionally helpful to me. Even if you don't share my particular belief, I believe you will still find help and comfort in what follows, since suffering is such a common language.

I know that God does not desire suffering for its own sake, nor is it His ultimate goal for me. When Adam rebelled against God in the Garden of Eden, human suffering entered the world. However, that didn't put God at a disadvantage. As a master artist, He was and is able to take the mess that is suffering and turn it into something beautiful. In the Bible, the book of James says, *"Consider it pure joy whenever you face trials of many kinds"*. This is God's consolation plan for suffering. Suffering seems like such a crummy way to spend an afternoon, or a month, or a season, or a life - so if there is any way to redeem that difficult time and turn it into something useful, then maybe the outcome of the suffering could be worth the pain of the experience.

However, this doesn't make suffering any more enjoyable in the moment. Suffering is terrible. In fact, if it isn't terrible, it isn't suffering. Suffering is a part of life on planet earth. It happens to everyone. But when it comes, it doesn't have to defeat us. God can and will use it to produce in us incredible and beautiful things.

As I said, I am writing this in the midst of a season of suffering. It is important to me to write this now, not when everything has worked out and all my questions have been answered. My desire is that "within" my struggle others can find hope. This is not a scholarly work. By that I mean that I haven't read extensively on the subject of suffering. Rather, I am simply sharing my perspectives and insights as I go through this season and as I marinate in God's Word, the Bible. So, join me as I share some of the conversations that I have had with God and my journeys in His Word, in my attempt to understand this road called suffering.

CHAPTER 1

BE CAREFUL WHAT YOU WISH FOR

We all know people that we admire – they are the people who have accomplished great things or have acted in great ways. The type of person I have found that I admire most is the one who endures great suffering and emerges unbroken. They are changed, but their spirit has endured.

Richard Wurmbrand, the founder of "The Voice of the Martyrs" was one such person. He spent many years in a communist prison being tortured for his faith, both physically and psychologically. I read several of his books and was shocked at the suffering he was made to endure. At one point, he spent three years in a cell buried twelve feet under ground with no lights or windows. There wasn't even any sound because the guards wore felt on the soles of their shoes. They would beat him, drug him, humiliate him and leave him in his despair. And yet, he endured. He writes that God met him in the midst of that horror. Shockingly, he forgave the guards and prayed for them, even while in his captivity.

Others fit that same bill: Corrie ten Boom, Nelson Mandela, Mother Teresa. When I hear their stories, I am inspired. I want to be just like them.

When I was in my 30's, I met Rhonda. She was suffering with significant physical ailments, and yet she had a certain personal quality that I deeply admired and respected. I believe that what so impressed me was how she suffered; the only way I can describe it is to say that she suffered with dignity. She wasn't a whiner or complainer; she suffered with grace and acceptance and courage…in a word: dignity. By this I don't mean that she just put on a brave face and pretended that nothing was wrong. I sometimes attempt that. I try to curtail the process, try to get to the end result without ever going through the middle. That path is inherently dishonest, and though it may impress a few people for a few moments, pretending the suffering away doesn't transform one's emotional or spiritual health. Rhonda didn't seem to walk that false way, rather, she lived through her pain honestly and humbly.

I felt honored to be her friend and to have conversations both inside and outside the suffering that she experienced. I saw her on good days and bad days. I observed her when optimism and hope came naturally and were easy to hang on to, and when they weren't. Through it all, I was very impressed by her and very humbled by her dignity.

I remember wishing that one day I, too, would be able to suffer with dignity.

Be careful what you wish for.

You see, I think there is only one way that I can learn to suffer with dignity, and that is to suffer. There is no other path. In fact, I find I typically start by suffering poorly, to an embarrassing degree. And then, hopefully, by God's grace, I suffer somewhat less poorly. And I continue suffering over and over, each time hopefully a bit less poorly than the time before.

I guess I would say that, for the most part, I had a relatively suffering-free upbringing. I mean, it wasn't as though everything went right in my life. I had struggles to be sure; teenage angst, financial stress, relationship tensions, personal failures; but, all things considered, my life was pretty good.

I grew up in a great family, with parents who loved me and siblings who were fun to be around. I was healthy. I enjoyed school and sports and friends. I had success in my jobs. I married a wonderful young woman and we started having kids. I had the privilege of working in the career that was my first choice. In a way, I felt like I had lived a charmed life. I remember thinking, with a certain amount of dread, that the other shoe had to drop some time soon.

And then, in 1998, the difficult times began in earnest. There are three main conditions under which I categorize most of my suffering: kidney disease, depression and stress disorder. Each has had varying degrees of impact on my life over the last fourteen years, and it seems I haven't had a prolonged period without experiencing the negative effects of at least one of these conditions.

SUFFERING POORLY

I suppose I wish that I could write about how well I handle suffering. Then everyone could cite me as an example of a person who suffered with dignity. But, alas, that is not the case.

Early in my journey of suffering, I discovered that I am naturally a pathetic sufferer. A whiner. Panicked and angry in those early days, I blamed and threatened God.

How's that for dignified?

I absolutely hated the fact that suffering had come knocking on my door (and remember, I had *wanted* to learn to suffer with dignity).

If I had to rate my ability to suffer with dignity, I was about equal to a spoiled two-year-old wanting a toy in a store.

I've seen those kids. And heard them. They scream bloody murder. Their faces are all red and puffy. They act like the worst affliction in the world, the greatest injustice ever thrust on anyone, is happening to them. Frankly, it is quite embarrassing for all involved. And yet, I was acting just like a spoiled kid.

I actually had the audacity to shake my fist at God and demand that He tell me just what He thought He was doing.

I remember when the first signs of my kidney disease showed up. It was a cold December morning and I had just gone out for a run. I had taken up running several years earlier and I loved hitting the road early in the morning. I had worked up to 16k on my long runs and was hoping to attempt a half marathon. That morning, I headed out on an 8k loop that I had named the "Ridge Run". It took me down a road that overlooked the small village of Chatsworth, Ontario and then through that village and back up the country road to our home. I loved this run.

The morning started as usual with me leaving the quiet house to greet my tail-wagging dog, Riley. Riley was my running partner and was eagerly anticipating our morning ritual. I stretched a bit, and then we were off. I remember thinking, as I was running, that I didn't feel quite right. I felt more sluggish than I should have, but I kept pushing through because I wasn't going to let a little tiredness dissuade me. By the time I got home, however, I was utterly exhausted. I tied the dog up, went inside and slumped in a chair. I could hardly move. Eventually I crawled up to bed and collapsed. I had a fever and I was completely spent. The next day I was no better, and by the third day I realized that something was definitely wrong.

I was shocked to realize that my legs were completely numb; I couldn't feel them at all. I couldn't walk. I had internal bleeding; my blood pressure was through the roof. Over the next six weeks I hardly got out of bed. It turned out that I had a strep virus that had resulted in IgA Nephropathy. I still don't understand all the ins and outs of the disease, but the end result of that initial onset was a loss of about 40% of my kidney function.

It didn't take long for me to begin my tirade against God. I was so angry. I remember writing a prayer to Him in which I said, "You can't do this to me. You can't take my strength away from me" (that is the cleaned up version). I was filled with doubt and disillusionment. I questioned His love and His care.

Thank God, He didn't write me off in those early days. Rather, He rolled up His sleeves and set out to complete the good work that He had begun in me. He was going to answer my wish; I was going to learn to suffer with dignity. To clarify, I don't mean to say that I believe God struck me with this suffering; rather, He allowed it, and then leaned heavily into leveraging it for my ultimate benefit.

It has been fourteen years since that first onset, and I am still learning. Some days it feels as though I have come a long way. Other days, it feels like I am still just coming home from that Ridge Run and learning about suffering for the first time. Often have I cried, "Have mercy on me, O God." He has always heard my cry.

Though I wanted quick results, the kind of character that God sought to develop in me could only be developed over a long period of time. I truly wanted to learn to be a good sufferer, but I was ready for suffering school to be out after the first week. I thank God that, in His mercy, He stuck with the program despite my short-sighted and frightened cries for relief.

CHAPTER 2

WHY IS THIS HAPPENING?

If I had a nickel for every time I asked "Why is this happening?" my financial pressures would be virtually non-existent.

That said, I do think this is a good and fair question…if I am asking it honestly and humbly. In fact, I have learned a lot by pondering that simple question. I have come to realize that when I ask it, there are two things I am hoping will be satisfied: my mind and my heart. For me, my inquiry is both an objective, intellectual question as well as a deeply personal, emotional question.

I have come to realize that there are actually several possibilities as to why this suffering has come to me. And like any good doctor or mechanic, I need to diagnose the problem before I can prescribe a solution; once I can identify a particular reason for a given instance of suffering, it can help me navigate my way through that suffering a little better, with purpose.

One Psalm that has been particularly instructive to me is Psalm 107. I love the poetry and symmetry of this Psalm. It describes four different groups of people. To help me remember them, I have given each group a name: LOSERS, REBELS, VICTIMS and FOOLS. To me, it seems that each group suffers for a particular reason. I find that when I consider my suffering through the lens of Psalm 107, it helps me know what my most appropriate response should be.

LOSERS (Psalm 107:4-5)

Some were wandering in desert wastelands with no place to settle. They were hungry and thirsty and their lives were wasting away.

I know the term "loser" has some negative connotations and calling a group of people losers just seems like an outright slur, but that is not how I am using it here. In this case, when I say loser I mean "people who seem to keep on losing."

It's a bit like the Little River Band's song, "Lonesome Loser."

Have you heard about the lonesome loser?
Beaten by the Queen of Hearts every time
Have you heard about the lonesome loser?
He's a loser but he still keeps on trying

These are the people who, when opportunity knocked on their door, were out at the grocery store getting milk. When at last their ship sailed in, it arrived an hour after they had opted to take the train. They just seem to miss their big break time and time again. I might just as well have called them "The Unfortunate" or "The Unlucky".

The Psalmist says that they are trying to find a place to settle, but are unsuccessful. They aren't sitting around waiting for relief to come to them, for the proverbial check to arrive in the mail, they are actively seeking a better situation. Yet it seems that the cards are stacked against them. No matter what they try, it's not working. I like this group of people. I can identify with them; my heart goes out to them.

I have often felt like I am in the LOSER category. I am trying to do whatever I can to remedy my difficult situation, but things just go from bad to worse. I think of the woman who had been subjected to bleeding for twelve years until she finally came to Jesus. Mark describes her situation this way, *"She had suffered a great deal under the care of many doctors and had spent all she had, yet instead of getting better, she grew worse."* I wonder how many times she cried out, "What am I doing wrong? Why isn't this getting any better?"

In the book of Ecclesiastes, Solomon described this same conundrum 3000 years ago. *"I saw something else meaningless under the sun. Righteous men get what the wicked deserve and wicked men get what the righteous deserve."*

This seems to me to be the most difficult of all the reasons for suffering, because it just doesn't make any sense. I love to solve things and fix things, but sometimes there's nothing I can do that will solve or fix the situation I am in.

REBELS (Psalm 107:10-12)

Some were prisoners suffering in chains because of their rebellion against God's commands.

At times, another reason for my suffering is because of punishment. I know that this can be a particularly troublesome thought. How can a loving God punish?

It says in the book of Hebrews,

"My son, do not make light of the Lord's discipline, and do not lose heart when he rebukes you, because the Lord disciplines those he loves, and he punishes everyone he accepts as a son."

(Hebrews 12:5-6)

This may be the easiest one to understand, but the hardest one to accept. It is easy because justice resonates in my heart; when someone does something wrong, they should be punished. And yet it is hard to accept because I do not like to admit that I have done anything wrong. Let me explain.

I get this very specific feeling when I am driving down the road and all of a sudden I see the flashing lights of a police car in my rear view mirror. It is a feeling that is both hot and cold at the same time. I am checking everything...my speed, my seatbelt, the bodies in the trunk (just kidding). Most of the time, the officer just pulls around me to catch some other villain, but sometimes it's me...and I hate it when that happens. It's awful, parked there on the side of the road with the police car behind me, lights all ablaze, screaming to the passing traffic, "Hey look at Tim! Tim was speeding! Can you believe that Tim was speeding? Shame on you, Tim!"

However, one time I noticed a radar trap on a busy road in our city and I had a great idea. I purchased a Root Beer float from the nearest A&W and then I sat across the street from the radar trap. I sipped my float and watched the officers pull over speeder after speeder. I can't begin to describe the joy I felt at that experience. Every time they would catch someone I was elated. It was like the best day fishing ever, getting strike after strike.

What did that tell me? I don't mind consequences for wrongdoing as long as they're not consequences for my wrongdoing. Well, that's not the way the game is played.

Sometimes my suffering is a direct result of punishment. There is a Lawgiver and Judge and when I break His law, I will be punished or disciplined. Now, when God punishes me it is not like He takes some morbid pleasure in my suffering. As a father, I have had to discipline my children. It has never been an enjoyable experience for me. In fact, it is the worst part about being a parent. That's why being a grandparent is going to be so much fun. I won't have to be the disciplinarian. It won't be my responsibility. I will get to do what I wanted to do with my kids all along: just love them and bless them and always be the good guy...and leave the discipline duties to someone else. But as a parent, that is my gig. The reason I discipline my kids is because I love them. I know that if certain behaviors are left unchecked, that precious child is going to be heading for an ocean of suffering in their future. If they think that they can lie and things will be better for them, they are going to be very sorry. Or if they think that it is appropriate to smack their siblings when they are mad, or to steal whatever they want, or to be disrespectful to the people around them, then their lives are going to be miserable.

So to help them, to set them up for a better future, I have the responsibility to discipline them. But it is love-based discipline. And that is how God treats me. Yes, there are times when I will need to be punished for something I have done wrong, but punishment is never the end result. It is always a love-based action from the Heavenly Father who loves me very much and wants to ensure that I have a life of joy and fullness.

I need to humbly repent of my suffering and turn away from doing it any more.

VICTIMS (Psalm 107:23-27)

Others went out on the sea in ships; they were merchants on the mighty waters.

The picture the Psalmist describes here is merchants traveling across the sea to carry out their business. In the course of their journey, they encountered a terrible storm. *In their peril their courage melted away. They reeled and staggered like drunken men; they were at their wits' end.*

Maybe I am reading into this a bit, but it seems to me that the merchants were at the mercy of the captain of the ship. They entrusted themselves to his wisdom. Obviously, storms come when storms come, but I wonder if there was a poor decision on the part of the ship's captain to sail in dangerous waters. It would seem then that the merchant's suffering was a result of the captain's decisions.

Sometimes, our suffering comes as a direct result of another's actions. This seems grossly unfair.

A spouse commits adultery.

A trusted adult abuses a child.

A coworker spreads malicious lies.

A drunk driver slams into a vehicle.

There is so much evil and wickedness in the world and it is unbelievably horrible what humans will do to each other.

Wouldn't it be better to just stop those people in their tracks? Why are people allowed to perpetrate such terrible things on the innocent? This is a difficult and complicated question, but I believe that it all comes down to our freedom to choose.

1. The ability to choose between good and evil is a direct result of the image of God in our lives.

The Bible says that we were created in the image of God. One of the markers of that image is our free will. This is what it means to be human. God could have created us like trees or rocks, with no ability to choose between good or evil. He could have made us like the other animals that function primarily out of instinct. If a wolf finds a fresh carcass of a deer, the wolf will eat. It doesn't consider not eating. It doesn't think about gathering other needy animals and sharing his find. He eats. This is how he was programmed. Humans have been given higher powers of choice than that wolf. This is one of the main characteristics that sets us apart as humans.

2. The ability to choose is the foundation of love.

I think the main reason we have free will is because God wanted us to experience the greatest gift of all: love. He could have caused us to act like we love Him; but that wouldn't really be love. People make people do all sorts of things. With the right amount of strength or coercion, a person can be made to do almost anything…but you can't make a person love. Love has to be freely given. God knew that love would be the most important and most powerful action in the world, and He wanted us to experience it. But in order to really experience love, we need the true freedom of choice.

3. The ability to choose means that a person can choose love.

We have been given the opportunity to experience the greatest depths of what it means to be human. There is no more beautiful thing than to love or be loved by another.

1 Corinthians 13 says, *"and now these three things remain: faith, hope and love. And the greatest of these is love."*

I have been loved by my parents, by my siblings, by my wife, by my children, by my friends…and that has been the greatest part of my life. I have also made the choice to love others, and those choices have filled my life with immeasurable depths of joy.

4. The ability to choose means that a person can choose to not love.

Giving humans free will was a highly risky venture, because it meant that our potential to choose evil was very real - as real as the potential to choose good. And everyone is given that choice. We live in a world where the option to not love is often chosen, and because of that there is very real and terrible suffering that exists. Yet the only way to prevent a man from choosing evil would be to also take away his option to choose love.

I know that my ability to choose love means that I also have the ability to not choose love…and, sadly, I have made that choice many times. I have chosen to put my agenda before the needs of others. I have chosen to take care of myself first. I have chosen to act or speak in ways that help me and harm others. Others have had to suffer as a result of my choices and my failures, and I should therefore not consider myself completely innocent when I suffer due to someone else's choices. We all have a hand in the problem. No one has lived a perfect life. We are all at fault.

FOOLS (Psalm 107:17-18)

Some became fools through their rebellious ways and suffered affliction because of their iniquities.

There is a fourth source of suffering that is somewhat humbling to admit: I am not as intelligent as I think I am. I put myself through so much discomfort simply because I make reckless, unintelligent decisions.

I remember working for my dad when I was a kid. He was a plumber. We were working on a new apartment complex and he needed me to get some metal couplings from the supply room. As I collected them, I discovered that I could slip these metal couplings around my arms like bracelets. They were about three inches wide and I was able to put seven or eight couplings on each of my eleven-year-old arms. I was pretty proud of myself. Not only was I able to transport more than a dozen couplings at a time, but I also looked like a cool, futuristic robot.

It was probably that "futuristic robot" concept that propelled me into the suffering I soon experienced. You see, as I was returning to my dad, my imagination was working at full capacity. I was swinging my arms, not as a human might, but as a futuristic robot might. And then, when I saw a large roll of metal wire, I knew that any futuristic robot worth his weight in metal would clearly have to jump it. I began to build up speed...super futuristic robot speed...and I hurled my incredible metal-glistening body towards the obstacle. With amazing grace and agility I leapt over the wire.

Two small details would have made the outcome at least somewhat less humiliating. First, if my left foot had cleared the wire with the rest of my body and second, if all the other trade workers hadn't been on break, with nothing else to do but sip their coffees and watch a maniacal metal-clad boy hurl himself to certain death.

The result was an overwhelming, astounding, ego-crushing wipe out. The sharp edges of the metal couplings dug into my arms; blood poured out. The tradesmen didn't know what to do. This was definitely something they had never witnessed before (but only because they had never worn couplings on their arms, I bet). My dad, of course, had to interrupt his work and get me all bandaged up. I still have the scars.

Foolishness. That's all it was.

We eat too much or drink too much or smoke too much and wonder why we have health issues.

We spend too much on things we want rather than on things we need and we wonder why we are suffering in financial stress.

We chase after some unreachable goal at work and sacrifice our relationships, our sanity, our souls, and then we wonder why we feel burnt out.

That was once my story. At one point in my life I had made a vow that I would be the best employee no matter what job I had. I had promised myself that no employer would ever have reason to be disappointed in me. Well, the extreme to which I took that obsession was just foolishness. That impossible standard drove me to exhaustion. It was pride-based, and competition-focused, and it meant that I spent too much energy chasing something that was unattainable. That is, my goal was not to be the best that I could be, but rather to be better than everyone else. This state of mind was highly stressful, and not what I was meant to do. The end result for me, in this case, was months and months of dark suffering with depression and stress disorder.

That said, we all suffer to some degree as a result of our own stupidity. That's just the way it is. This is our first time through this life. We will romance wrongly and parent wrongly and work wrongly. But we can learn from our mistakes. We can make changes. And those changes can bring a reduction in suffering.

LOSERS, REBELS, VICTIMS and FOOLS represent four common reasons why I suffer. Yet, there is a fifth reason that I see in Psalm 107. It isn't as explicitly stated as the first four, but it is apparent nonetheless. It is introduced in the first verse and it permeates the entire Psalm.

Give thanks to the LORD, for he is good; his love endures forever.

I call this fifth group the **BELOVED**. Sometimes, it is because of God's great love for me that I suffer.

But shouldn't true love eradicate suffering? If God really cared about me, shouldn't He save me from my difficulties?

I played basketball in high school. My coach, Mr. B, made us suffer. We had to run lines and do wall jumps until we felt like throwing up. We had to practice offensive plays and defensive tactics over and over. He seemed merciless towards us, unmoved by our cries for relief. Why did he do this? Was he a wicked tyrant, exulting in our pain and misery? No, he believed that we could be better ball players, and he was going to help us reach our full potential.

Philippians says, *"He who began the good work in you will carry it on to completion…"*

God sees my true potential and He will work tirelessly in the direction of seeing that potential realized. This is what love does: it toils tirelessly to see us become all that we were meant to be.

BELOVED also means that I love, and love compels me to suffer where I otherwise might not have. Again, in Philippians, Paul says, *"it has been granted to you, on behalf of Christ, not only to believe in Him, but also to suffer for Him."* He goes on later to say, *"I want to know Christ and the power of His resurrection, and the fellowship of sharing in His sufferings…"*

I had a friend who worked with an organization that reached out to troubled inner-city teens. He worked there for many years. During those years he was robbed, threatened, lied to and slandered. He often had to go without, yet he constantly shared what little he had. This was not an easy life, but he chose it and pursued it with all his heart. Why? Because he was compelled by love. He chose a life of suffering because of his love for Jesus.

Jesus said, *"Whoever wants to be my disciple must deny themselves and take up their cross and follow me."*

Being a part of the mission of Jesus is no walk in the park. Suffering will come as a result of being His disciple, but the final payoff will be worth every ounce of pain. Sometimes it is simply love that compels us to suffer. Jesus does not ask us to do anything that He Himself would not do. In fact, He suffered more than any of us will ever suffer. He did this for love.

CHAPTER 3

WHY IS THIS HAPPENING...TO ME?

I love memorizing scripture. One of my ambitions is to memorize and retain as much scripture as I can until the day I die. One of the books I have memorized is Ecclesiastes. In 2006, I worked with director Val Lieske and we created a one-man show called, "Before the Silver Cord is Severed", in which I dramatically present the book of Ecclesiastes (you can check it out on YouTube). God gave me many opportunities to perform the show in churches, at a Christian University, at Fire Exit Theatre in Calgary, and at the Calgary Fringe Festival. Almost 10,000 people saw "Silver Cord". Whenever I was asked what was next for the show, I always said that my greatest desire was to perform it in a secular university. I believed that God's Word could more than stand up to the scrutiny of intelligent skeptics, but I had no idea how I might get into a university.

Then, in 2011, my brother Michael, who is a professor at Purdue University in Indiana, brokered an opportunity for me to perform the show there. All at once, God made the impossible possible. I was overwhelmed with thankfulness for His kindness in granting me the desire of my heart.

By February, I had signed the contract, bought the plane tickets and made all the necessary reservations; a September show was in the bag. Then came May, and sickness. As a result of the steroids I had been taking for my kidney disease and my recurring gout, I ended up with diverticulitis. The antibiotics I was taking for the diverticulitis caused a bacterial imbalance in my intestines (wiped out my natural gut flora) and resulted in a Clostridium

Difficile (or C. diff) infection. Needless to say, I was completely wiped out physically and emotionally by the end of that ordeal. In addition, we would later discover that I had severe Sleep Apnea (my heart was actually flat-lining ninety times an hour - over seven hundred times a night). I woke up each morning as tired as I had been when I went to bed the night before. With this perfect storm of medical setbacks, my history of stress disorder came back to visit me with a vengeance. I could not handle being around anyone but my wife and my kids. Even the smallest amount of contact with anyone else left me exhausted, nauseous and shaking uncontrollably.

I knew that I had to make a decision regarding the Purdue show, and I set a deadline of June 15th for my final answer. In my current state, I knew there was no way I could talk to the stewardess on the plane, much less perform "Silver Cord" in front of a crowd. I begged God to heal me and in my heart I knew He would. It was obvious that He had opened a door for me to present "Silver Cord" at Purdue; somehow, He was going to restore my strength. But May came and went, and the first few days of June were soon checked off the calendar. Nothing was changing with my health situation, and I was growing concerned that maybe God hadn't heard my pleas.

At last the fateful day arrived, and with great disappointment and disillusionment I realized that I had to cancel the show. That day was devastating to me. I couldn't believe that God hadn't "come through". It made absolutely no sense. My stunned prayers became accusatory in nature.

"God, what happened? Why would you do this to me? Is it because there is a long line-up somewhere of people who love to memorize Your Word and translate it into meaningful, dramatic recitations? Am I so redundant that You can just callously bench me without notice?"

I was hurt and confused. I felt I had a strong and compelling case for why this bad thing should not happen to me. And as it turned out, this wouldn't be the only disappointment I was to experience.

Several months previously, our church had begun a campaign to raise money and we were all asked to make pledges. I had been a part of these types of campaigns throughout my life and I had always contributed. In the past, I tried to give sacrificially based on what I determined I could scrape together, but I had never given beyond that. This time, I felt that God was urging me to give in faith, to make a pledge that I would only be able to fulfill if He worked a miracle. So, with great anticipation and joy, my wife, Jennifer, and I made a pledge that was easily double any pledge that we had ever made before. Almost immediately, we received an unexpected inheritance from an aunt of mine, and we gave a significant portion of that towards meeting the pledge. I was elated. This is what walking by faith must be like, I thought.

Fast forward to May 2011 when sickness, disappointment, and frustration were slowly overtaking me. Because of my inability to function in social settings, I couldn't work; I had to go on long term disability. Suddenly, our income wasn't what it used to be, though of course our bills kept their steady pace. After a full year of this financial unrest, a terrifying reality began to settle on our hearts: we might lose the house, we might lose everything.

How could this happen to me? How could I be struggling so severely in the area of finances when I was making such huge strides forward in my faith and trust in God regarding money? I remember reading stories of faithful saints who would write a check for a particular need, not knowing where the money would come from to cover it, but God would always miraculously provide. I felt that my check to God had bounced, and not only did my act of faith now seem useless, but I also got dinged with a twenty-five dollar penalty from the bank.

Have you ever felt this way? You are doing everything right, you are being obedient to God, and yet He seems to be taking morbid pleasure in rewarding that obedience with pain. This is a complex and confusing place to be. What are the options for my response?

Well, I could just go with the easiest first option that comes to mind, that God is simply a cruel deity who cares not for me at all. At first blush, this would seem to explain the situation. The result of that option, however, is to be filled with bitterness and rage against Him and want nothing more to do with Him. I have met many people who have chosen this option and, while it seems to resolve the immediate problem, the consequences of abandoning faith in God leave one in a soul-destructive state of mind.

A second option is to believe that God is simply a figment of my imagination. He is something made up by weak people to help them make sense of the world. Bad things happen to good people and good things happen to bad people, not because God's nature is questionable, but rather because there is no God. I am merely acting the fool when I try to attribute joy and pain, suffering and relief to an all-powerful Other. I have atheist friends who will tell me that they have no issue with God personally, because there simply is no personal God. Again, this option would seem to answer some of the quandaries of the immediate situation. The problem is, this mindset raises a host of other issues.

A final option would be to believe that my arguments against God might be faulty, and that His existence and His love can coexist with pain, suffering and apparent injustice. Humbly accepting how little I seem to know about most things, this third option actually seems to make the most sense. So, I call out to God again.

> *Me: God, why do bad things happen to good people?*

> *God: Good question.   I have two more. First, what exactly do you mean by "good people" and second,   why do good things happen to good people?*

What *do* I mean by "good" people?   I suppose I mean people who are not "bad" people. Bad people are people who steal from the weak and helpless, who murder and rape and bully. Bad people make society unbearable.   Therefore, anyone who doesn't steal, murder, rape or bully must be a good person. I don't steal, murder, rape or bully, therefore I must be a good person - a bona fide, card-carrying good person.

But is that a correct and reasonable conclusion?

God's Word is a bit more direct in its definition of good. In the most famous sermon of all time, the Sermon on the Mount (found in Matthew 5-7), Jesus describes a good person. He agreed with my assessment that it is wrong to murder and commit adultery, but He takes it one step further (one HUGE step further, actually).

"You have heard that it was said, 'do not murder', and anyone who murders is subject to judgment. But I tell you, anyone who is angry with his brother is subject to judgment."

"You have heard that it was said, 'do not commit adultery'. But I tell you, anyone who looks at a woman lustfully has already committed adultery with her in his heart."

To add to that, in the book of James it says, *"If you really keep the royal law found in Scripture, 'Love your neighbor as yourself,' you are doing right. But if you show favoritism, you sin and are convicted by the law as lawbreakers. For whoever keeps the whole law and yet stumbles at just one point is guilty of breaking all of it. For he who said, 'Do not commit adultery,' also said, 'Do not murder.' If you do not commit adultery but do commit murder, you have become a lawbreaker."*

And, just in case there is still any doubt, Paul writes in Romans:

"There is no one righteous, not even one."

He goes on to state emphatically, *"All have sinned and have fallen short of the glory of God."*

If karma was the measuring stick for goodness, surely I wouldn't stand a chance. True, I can honestly attest that I have never murdered, but have I hated? Have I lusted or gossiped? Have I acted out of pride or jealousy or bitterness? Have I lost my temper? Have I said hurtful things? Have I tried to push my agenda through at the expense of stepping on others? Of course I have, and not just once; this could be a fairly accurate general description of my nature. When stated that way, I have to accept that I am really not a good person at all. Left unchecked, those negative actions and attitudes will make society unbearable. I realize that this must be one of the reasons why there is so much pain in the world, because people like me are allowed to wander about unhindered. The problem with trying to use a scale to measure my good actions against my bad actions is that I am extremely lenient with myself and, therefore, my final assessment can't help but be questionable and, therefore, unreliable. I want so desperately to be justified that I will make generous allowances for myself so that my "score card" will appear passable even if it is not exactly true.

In the book of Job, Job says to God, *"I have sinned, I have perverted what is right, but I did not get what I deserved. God has delivered me from going down to the pit, and I shall live to enjoy the light of life."* (Job 33:27-28).

Psalm 103 says, *"God does not treat us as our sins deserve or repay us according to our iniquities."* If we were treated as our sins deserved we wouldn't be able to endure.

So, the bigger question is not, 'why do bad things happen to good people?' but rather, 'why do good things happen'? What did I ever do to deserve the kind of wife that I have who loves me and has stuck with me for the last twenty-five years? Why would someone like me, with all my faults, be able to have such great relationships with my children? How much good did I do to earn being born into the wealth of Canada and not the poverty of Mumbai? I may lose my house, but what did I ever do to deserve a house to lose? My health may be poor, but what did I ever do to deserve good health in the first place? Some fellow North American will say, "Everyone deserves good health" or "everyone deserves a house." Really? Take a look around. Ninety percent of the world's population has less than we do here in North America. Why is that? Are we so much better as people that we deserve our comfort and riches? Absolutely not! I have met incredibly humble and amazing people in some of the worst places on the planet. If we were to use an accurate scale, they would put my goodness to shame.

Here's the truth: every good thing I have comes solely from the kindness and grace of God. As Bono so aptly put it, "Grace trumps Karma every time".

My friend Cam sent me this thought via Facebook, "Good things happen to bad people. I am not bitter. I just don't know why God would allow those good things to happen to me!"

Instead of expending most of my energy complaining to God about why this bad thing is happening to me, I am much better served by giving thanks for all the good things He has done for me. This is what I am discovering: the list of the bad things in my life, no matter how exhaustive I make it, is always finite, but the list of the good things is unending.

And so, despite the struggles I am experiencing, I embrace the fact that I have a choice, and I choose to give thanks. I choose to see the good, for it is there. And in choosing to see the good, I am able to endure the bad because I am overwhelmed at the inexplicable kindness of a loving God.

CHAPTER 4

WHERE IS GOD?

Me: God, I am extremely concerned about the future. I don't know what I am supposed to do.
God: I am not as concerned
Me: Can't you tell me what will happen so I know it will be okay?
God: What if I just tell you that it will be okay?
Me: What am I supposed to do now?
God: This is good.
Me: (silent)
God: I love you. I have not forgotten you. You are exactly in the center of My care. It will be okay.

I think I am fairly realistic in my hopes and expectations. I don't wish irresponsibly. Of course, a million dollars would be a real help in my life, but I don't wish for that. Absolutely, I would love to be able to slam dunk a basketball, but I don't wish for that either. There are both ways to earn money and ways to improve my vertical that don't require prayers being offered up to heaven. However, there are other times when what I am wishing for is good, and needed, and even God-honoring. I try my best to accomplish those things, but when my best just isn't enough I cry out to God for help.

I tell Him that I will do most of the work, I will cross the t's and dot the i's, and that I will cover as many of the bases as possible. I try to limit His responsibilities to just one thing. One tiny, simple thing that we both know only He can do. After all, I don't want to overwhelm Him; He does have quite a lot on His plate.

So, I set it all up, do my bit, toss Him the ball and then wait for Him to do His bit. And…He doesn't. I panic. I reconsider all the options. I come up with a contingency plan. Oh, it's not as good as the first plan, but it will suffice. Again, I scramble to get things all set up for Him and again I toss Him the ball. Once more it hits Him in the chest and bounces uselessly to the ground. He doesn't even try to catch it. And in that moment, I am terribly confused.

What's the big problem? Would it really hurt so much for Him to toss me a bone out of His boundless wealth? Could He not brush even a few crumbs off His extravagantly laid table?

In the book of 1 Kings, there is a confrontation between Elijah and the 850 prophets of the gods Baal and Asherah. It was a showdown at high noon. It was Wyatt Earp and Doc Holliday against the outlaw cowboys at the OK Corral. The point of the confrontation was to prove, once and for all, whose God was real and whose was not.

The rules were simple. Choose an ox, prepare it for sacrifice, lay it out on an altar and then call on God. The god who answered by fire would thereby be revealed as the real God. Elijah let the prophets go first. They chose their ox, prepared it for sacrifice and then began to call on Baal. They did this throughout the morning, but nothing happened. No response from Baal, no fire from heaven.

We pick up the story in 1 Kings 18:27 (MSG):

By noon, Elijah had started making fun of them, taunting, "Call a little louder—he is a god, after all. Maybe he's off

*meditating somewhere or other, or maybe he's gotten involved in
a project, or maybe he's on vacation. You don't suppose he's
overslept, do you, and needs to be waked up?" They prayed
louder and louder, cutting themselves with swords and knives—a
ritual common to them—until they were covered with blood. This
went on until well past noon. They used every religious trick and
strategy they knew to make something happen on the altar, but
nothing happened—not so much as a whisper, not a flicker of
response.*

I remember reading this as a kid and cheering for Elijah.
"That's right," I would say. "You prophets of Baal are getting it
handed to you today." But now, in my time of suffering and
need, my experience seems eerily similar to those prophets. I
pray louder and louder. I use every religious trick and strategy I
can think of, but nothing happens -- not so much as a whisper, not
a flicker of response.

So, what then? Do Elijah's words apply to me as well?
Has my God gotten involved in another project or is He off
meditating somewhere or on vacation? Maybe He's actually
asleep at the wheel. Maybe no one is minding the store after all.

Even though I know this is untrue, it is honestly how I feel
at times.

When I write fiction, I try to create interesting characters
that go on epic adventures and experience transformational life
challenges. I love my characters, but I am sure if they could talk
to me, they would question that love. You see, I can do anything
to them, make life as difficult as possible for them, because I
know how the story will end. I know that they will grow and be
able to handle the disaster. I am not at all concerned about their
final outcome because I know everything will be fine. In fact, it

is through those difficult times that my characters will come to the great end that I am envisioning for them.

The best stories are those in which real characters go through real suffering; the greater the suffering the greater the story. I would be bored out of my mind if I had to read a story where the protagonist doesn't suffer anything significant. Take for example this story of Bill:

Bill dreamt of marrying a beautiful woman and living in a nice house. Bill met and married Cathy. She is a beautiful woman. They live in a nice house.

The End

Yawn. Oh excuse me, I dozed off there.

It matters very much to me that terrible, difficult things happen to the characters in stories that I read, but I absolutely hate it when those things happen to me. I want my life to be like Bill's. Simple. Pain-free.

And the problem with living in a rich, free country is that we can live under the illusion that we can actually keep suffering at bay. I don't like cold so I turn up the heat in my house. I don't like the feeling of hunger so I run out to a fast food restaurant. I don't like feeling alone so I power up my computer, or turn up the volume on my flat screen TV.

We are a cushioned society in many ways. It's why suffering seems like such a shock to our systems; it feels like a personal affront to the comfort we have come to assume we deserve. Why else would I think that I have the right to question

God? I am the clay in the potter's hands that says, "Why are you forming me this way? I know better. Do it my way." It is an astounding act of arrogance to speak this way. I don't even know what will happen tomorrow and yet I presume to tell an all-knowing God what is best for my life? It would be laughable if it wasn't so wretched.

He is the writer of my story and He tells me that He loves me. Either I believe that or I don't. If I say I believe it, then I must act accordingly.

In the book of Mark, there are two accounts of Jesus' disciples getting caught in storms out on the lake. In the first account, a terrible storm comes and it appears that their boat is going to sink. Jesus is sleeping on a cushion in the boat. They panic. They wake Him up and accuse Him of not caring for them. He calms the storm with a word from His mouth and then asks them, "Why are you so afraid? Do you still have no faith?"

Their terror forced Jesus to resort to Plan B, the miraculous calming of the storm. And if Plan B was so spectacular, it makes me wonder what Plan A was going to be!

A second time, Jesus sent the disciples out on the lake. A great storm came and they were caught in the middle of it. Jesus was up on the hillside overlooking the lake and could see the disciples struggling at the oars. Like the first account, it didn't appear that He was doing anything to help them. After several hours of this, Jesus finally goes out to them, walking on the water. When they see Him, they are understandably freaked out, thinking He was a ghost. But Jesus gets into the boat with them and, again, the storm miraculously stops. This time, however, there is no questioning of their faith. I think they learned something between the two storms. Jesus could be trusted. He always has a plan and He is always aware of what is going on. Their response in the middle of the storm is not to cry out in fear, but rather to put their heads down and endure.

This is the lesson that I am trying to learn. I am loved and cared for. He has not forgotten me. The most important thing is that He is thinking of me, loves me, and has a plan for me. That plan could mean fifteen months off work or three years off work. That plan could include me being restored to full health and never having to suffer like this again. It could mean being restored to a degree of health with some very real limitations on what I am able to do. It could mean that I enter a season of health upswing only to enter another season of health downswing in the future.

In the end, it doesn't really matter. God will not allow anything in my life that could not be used for my benefit.

Paul says in Romans 8, *"We know that in all things, God works for the good of those who love Him, who are called according to His purpose."*

And God's idea of good is often quite different from my idea of good. My idea is remarkably unimaginative: money, comfort and ease. God's idea of good has more to do with my character and His glory. So, I want to quietly endure. When panic starts to well up in my heart, I want to speak a different word. God can be trusted. He knows what is best. I will wait on Him.

CHAPTER 5

WHAT HEALING CAN NEVER ACCOMPLISH

I remember when I was first hit by my kidney disease. I had been on a bit of a professional roll. I was getting opportunities to lead music and speak at bigger and bigger events. Everything seemed to be going along just like it said in Psalm 1: *"His delight is in the law of the Lord, and on His law he meditates day and night. He is like a tree planted by streams of water, which yields its fruit in season and whose leaf does not wither. Whatever he does prospers."*

But then, all at once, everything changed; I was taken out of the game. I felt less like a tree planted by streams of water and more like one planted in the middle of the Trans Canada highway, just trying to suck as much water from the unyielding pavement as I could. I remember distinctly feeling that the flow of success was rushing by me and all I could do was watch it pass.

I use to love walking in Harrison Park in Owen Sound, Ontario. Strolling along the Sydenham River was an experience of pure peace and delight. At several spots, the river water would pool off to the side, creating small ponds of still water. It lay there placidly while the rest of the river surged on by. I felt like that was now what was happening to me. Because of my physical infirmities, I had been subjected to stagnation. Everyone else seemed to be moving along happily and all I could do was watch them pass by.

It is always easiest for me to see what I am missing when I am suffering; the list formulates in my mind with very little effort.

-I am not able to work

-I am not able to contribute to the cause

-I am not able to make as much money as I once   did

-I am not able to do the things I love

-I am not the strong person I have always been

And because this list is so forthcoming, I can be quick to question God's love and kindness in my life. But God has been showing me something new. I am beginning to see all the things I would miss if I were healed.

HUMILITY

But he gives us more grace. That is why Scripture says: "God opposes the proud but gives grace to the humble." Submit yourselves, then, to God. Resist the devil, and he will flee from you. Come near to God and he will come near to you. Wash your hands, you sinners, and purify your hearts, you double-minded. Grieve, mourn and wail. Change your laughter to mourning and your joy to gloom. Humble yourselves before the Lord, and he will lift you up. (James 4:6-10)

Most, if not all, of the sin and brokenness in my life can be traced back to the one sin of pride. I don't know if this is true of everyone, though I have a hunch that it is. I have a deep desire to make sure that I am happy, honored, fulfilled, respected, appreciated, remembered, and successful. As a result, I am threatened easily. I can be passionately territorial. I constantly question my self-worth and my place in the world. It has been the source of most of the pain in my marriage. It has kept me from accepting and celebrating others as much as I could have. It has even stopped me from listening to the urging of God in my life.

Therefore, the kindest thing God could ever do for me would be to help me reduce my pride quotient, to take me down, not just several, but many sets of notches.

God has gifted me in several ways. I am an engaging public speaker, a decent musician and a creative dreamer. I have been a recording artist, actor, inventor and author of fictional works. It can become easy to rely on myself and my abilities, as though they came from me and are for the expansion of my fame. Oh yes, I say I need God, but that can be more theoretical than actually lived out. So, God, in His mercy, takes away those things I am so tempted to trust and rely on. Suddenly, I am left with none of those things. In very real ways, I am broken. I discover, quite painfully, that those gifts of God were never meant to take His place in my life. The resulting brokenness is not lovely at first. On the contrary, it is deeply humiliating. But humility is like the cough syrup Buckleys: "It tastes awful. And it works!"

It is only in humility that we are lifted up by God. In fact, pride is opposed by God. I don't know about you, but life is hard enough without having God opposing me. I need as much grace as I can get, and God promises that He will give that to me if I am humble. When I don't have the ability on my own to be humble, God helps the process along by allowing suffering to have its effect in my life.

DEPENDENCE

In you, O LORD, I have taken refuge; let me never be put to shame. Rescue me and deliver me in your righteousness; turn your ear to me and save me. Be my rock of refuge, to which I can always go. (Psalm 71:1-3)

I just read an article about the top twenty-five self-made men in American history. These were men, the article contended, who with no help from any outside source, pulled themselves up from lowly beginnings to fabulously wealthy and influential endings. Naturally, there was a lot of feedback on the article about who had been excluded from the list or who shouldn't have been included on the list. But at the end of it all, there was still a collection of men who were, seemingly universally, accepted as being "self-made".

This idea of being self-made is interesting to me. I confess that it is an ideal that pulls at my heart often. I want to be recognized not only as a person of substance, but also as a person who deserved that substance. I don't particularly like the idea of being indebted to anyone. But there are reasons to doubt that being self-made is possible, or is even a worthy goal.

Don't get me wrong, I believe in hard work and perseverance, but there is something highly erroneous about the term "self-made". Not only does it seem to imply an attitude of great arrogance, but it also signifies loneliness and a lack of appreciation for anyone else. I mean, come on. For every self-made man, there was a selfless mother who cared and changed and fed him at a time when he was most vulnerable. There were people along the way who spoke timely or encouraging words.

There were opportunities afforded to him by mere geography. And over it all, there was a God who created him, gifted him, and allowed him to experience all that he experienced.

Every once in a while, I experience little "hits" of self-made and, when I do, it immediately separates me from those around me; I feel superior to them, I feel like I don't need them. It also separates me from God. I think about Him less. I rely on Him less.

This is madness. My every breath comes from Him, and yet I am so ready to distance myself from Him. For this reason, I am so thankful for suffering. Suffering helps me to see what is real. Suffering peels back the illusion of self-security and reveals to me the true vistas of my need for God. When I hear new reports about my declining health or see the despairing truths about my financial situation, it is wholly without difficulty that I throw myself on the mercy of God. Yet, when I come to accept a new level of physical limitation or I move a few steps away from the edge of financial collapse, it doesn't take long before I can sense my heart saying, "I can do this on my own now."

Ultimately, there is no hope for eternal life apart from the mercy and grace of God. I am utterly dependent on Him for the things that matter the most. Anything that helps me see that reality more clearly is a gift. Anything that blurs or dulls that vision is a curse. Suffering washes away the grime on my windshield so that I can most clearly see the road ahead.

COMFORT

Blessed are those who mourn, for they will be comforted. (Matthew 5:4)

I first met Jennifer, my wife-to-be, in September of 1985. We attended the same college in Regina, Saskatchewan. One of our earliest times together was at Wascana Park, the beautiful grounds in the heart of Regina. We were there with a few of her friends on a warm September night. I felt so alive in her presence. I was 19 years old, and clearly enamored with her. Walking up the grassy expanse towards the parliament buildings I was suddenly filled with the urge to run. I challenged the others to a race and sped off like a…well, like a gazelle, I guess. Life coursed through my veins like a high speed train as I bounded across the field. I felt like Eric Liddle, the main character in the movie *Chariots of Fire*; I could feel God's pleasure on me as I ran. It should have been a beautiful moment. In fact, it could have been, except that I failed to negotiate properly the four-inch drop to the pavement at the end of the field. One moment, I was racing effortlessly, the next, I was skidding on the palms of my hands along the rough ground. As quickly and with as much decorum as I could salvage, I pulled myself up onto the steps of the Legislative building. Blood was pouring out of my shredded hands. The others came up and, with great concern, asked how I was doing. I told them I was okay, but it was a lie. I just wanted the bleeding to stop and the pain to recede.

Despite that humiliating and painful disaster, the rest of the evening turned out much better. Jennifer paid special attention to me. Her concern was better than any salve on my hands. She sat next to me as we watched the northern lights fill the Saskatchewan sky, attentive and protective.

God promises that He will comfort those who mourn. His comfort touches that deepest longing in our hearts to know that we are not alone, that we matter, that we are loved. There is no need for Him to show His tender comfort and care if we are not mourning. This is why Jesus said that we are blessed if we mourn. When I suffer, I will be comforted. This doesn't mean that God causes me to suffer just so that He can show me His comfort. That would be as absurd as Jennifer tripping me while I ran just so she could show concern for me after. But when I suffer, His comfort is immediately available.

Suffering is never pleasant. In July 2012, I fell to what felt like my lowest point ever. After over a year of praying to God to heal me or at least explain to me what was going on, I had finally grown exhausted of His apparent silence. It was a dark time of doubt and hopelessness, but God's love and kindness reached into the midst of my bleakness. He gently reminded me of His unending presence and affirmed to me that He had not forgotten me. Slowly, but surely, my spirits began to lift. He was the strong refuge to which I could always run. I memorized Psalm 71 during that time and repeated it over and over again.

> *In You, oh Lord, I have taken refuge;*
> *Let me never be put to shame*
> *Rescue me and deliver me in Your righteousness*
> *Turn Your ear to me and save me.*
> *Be my Rock of Refuge to which I can always go*
> *Give the command to save me*
> *For You are my refuge and my fortress*

Every pain-filled exhale of breath was a cry of that Psalm to God. He comforted me. He cared for me.

EMPATHY

Praise be to the God and Father of our Lord Jesus Christ, the Father of compassion and the God of all comfort, who comforts us in all our troubles, so that we can comfort those in any trouble with the comfort we ourselves have received from God. For just as the sufferings of Christ flow over into our lives, so also through Christ our comfort overflows. (1 Corinthians 1:3-5)

In the past, when I discovered that someone suffered from depression, I mostly stayed clear of them. It was not that I didn't care for them, I just didn't understand it. I had a label in my mind for those kinds of people; I assumed that they were weak, and if they just changed their way of thinking, things would get better for them. How ignorant. How insensitive.

Then God allowed me to suffer with depression. Suddenly, against my own will, and despite all the positive effort I could muster, I could barely go on. I remember a speaking engagement I had at a junior high youth retreat. I sat alone in an upstairs room while one floor below, five hundred eager young people were gathering for the meeting. I suddenly realized that I didn't want to leave that room. More than that, I didn't know if I *could* leave the room, and I wondered what would happen if they couldn't locate me. I just wanted to remain hidden away, sequestered in my secret lair. God helped me go through with my commitment, and over the next several months, He helped me cope with this new found infirmity, though it was a hard and difficult road to walk.

Something had changed in me, though; I had a new understanding and empathy for others who suffered from depression. I was able to use the comfort that I received from God, through His Word and through the love of those around me, to comfort others who were depressed.

This has proven true with each new difficulty I have encountered in my life; new windows of understanding and care have opened for others who suffer in similar ways. I don't necessarily believe that God allows me to suffer just so I will gain empathy, but I do believe that it is one of the beautiful ways He redeems suffering. By going through my own suffering, I have become a kinder, more understanding person. Suffering is making me look more and more like the God I love and serve.

HOPE

Not only so, but we also rejoice in our sufferings, because we know that suffering produces perseverance; perseverance, character; and character, hope. And hope does not disappoint us, because God has poured out his love into our hearts by the Holy Spirit, whom he has given us. (Romans 5:3-5)

Hope is the tiny bud on the wintry barren branch of suffering. Where there is no branch, there is no bud. Where there is no suffering, there is no hope. "Who hopes for what he already has?" The only time I hope is when I am "without", and suffering is nothing if not a season of being without.

There is an exhilarating feeling for many in the days leading up to Christmas. My kids, like lots of other kids, count down the days with eager anticipation. They have a hope of surprise and delights on Christmas morning. It is magical and wonderful. Some people call it "the Christmas Spirit". It affects how we live. Likewise, hope does this. It is a brilliant beckoning glimmer in an otherwise dark landscape. It fuels determination, disallowing me to surrender to my circumstance. Hope calls me to pursue and achieve heights I would never otherwise know.

In the end, suffering points me to the ultimate hope of heaven. There will come a time when God will wipe away every tear from our eyes. There will be no more death or mourning or suffering or pain. When my life is suffering-free, I tend to let up on my view and hope of heaven; in other words, I begin to live under the false pretense that this world is all there is. In subtle and not-so-subtle ways, this will cause me to live less of a life than when I am focused on eternity. Solomon says, "For death is the destiny of every man, the living should take this to heart" (Ecclesiastes 7:2).

Recently, I wrote in my journal this thought regarding hope:

Hope is interesting. It is precious. It is elusive. I woke this morning to discover that sometime during the night it had slipped from my grasp. But God, in His mercy, wrangled it for me and brought it back.

"Here," He said. "You lost this. Hold on tight."

STRENGTH

Three times I pleaded with the Lord to take [the infirmity] away from me. But he said to me, "My grace is sufficient for you, for my power is made perfect in weakness." Therefore I will boast all the more gladly about my weaknesses, so that Christ's power may rest on me. That is why, for Christ's sake, I delight in weaknesses, in insults, in hardships, in persecutions, in difficulties. For when I am weak, then I am strong. (2 Corinthians 12:8-10)

I bought myself a little 1995 pickup truck for $400. I knew that I would have to do some work on it. There was a disturbing rattle coming from the drive shaft, the thermostat was broken, and it needed a new windshield. It ran okay, but I wanted it to run better. So, after watching a few Youtube videos, I went to work taking out the old and putting in the new. I have since also changed the starter, the battery and the battery wire connectors. I am not a great mechanic, but I know enough that if something is broken, it needs to be replaced. I didn't just add another drive shaft to my truck; there was only room for one. I had to remove the old one to accommodate the new one. Each time I replaced the old for the new, the truck improved.

This is similar to our lives. We start out with a set of skills and abilities to handle the life we have been given. Some have a bigger skill set than others, but we all have a degree of natural abilities. However, God is interested in helping us become more than that; He wants to fill us with His strength. In a perfect world, I would allow Him to do that, but I am stubborn and want to trust my own strength. I am proud of myself and am unwilling to admit that I need help, even though I know I would be more effective if I had God's strength working through me.

Suffering tends to force the issue. When I can no longer rely on my abilities I cry out to God, and He fills me with his strength. I have supernatural encouragement and hope and endurance. For a year and a half, I have been on a sickness-induced house arrest. I am not speaking in front of thousands of people, I am not leading any organizations, I am not playing music anywhere. I can barely handle being with people for more than a half an hour. In many ways, I feel like I am of no use to anyone. However, the upside is that every day I cast myself on God's mercy and ask Him to use me and to work in me any way He chooses. I am constantly pleasantly surprised (though I probably shouldn't be) when someone tells me that God is using me to be a blessing and inspiration in their life. I wonder how that is even possible; I am not doing anything. But God is bigger than my weakness and can work not only just as well, but better than when I am strong. Does this mean that the strengths that He has given me are wasted? Not at all. Rather, my strengths can be infused with His strength, even as my weaknesses are. My reliance is on God, not on my strengths.

Paul says in Colossians 1, *"I pray...that you might be strengthened with all power according to His glorious might so that you might have great endurance and patience."*

This is what I want: not just the ability to endure or to be patient, but to have great endurance and great patience. Life is very difficult and only great endurance and patience will suffice.

MATURITY

Consider it pure joy, my brothers, whenever you face trials of many kinds, because you know that the testing of your faith develops perseverance. Perseverance must finish its work so that you may be mature and complete, not lacking anything. (James 1:2-4)

God has placed in us the desire to be better, to improve. This is His objective for our lives. It says in Philippians 1:6,

"For He who began the good work in you will carry it on to completion." God wants me to become complete. Currently, I am a long way from that. True, I am closer than I was ten years ago, but the road ahead is still long. However, I know that God is going to see to it that I continue towards that end until the day I die. And I believe that suffering is His chief means to accomplish that goal. In fact, I don't know if I grow at all apart from suffering.

Who needs to persevere when things are great? I don't need to persevere through a plate of nachos while watching a great movie. I don't need to persevere when everything is coming up roses. The only time I need to persevere is when things are horrible.

When I go work out in the gym, the goal is to put strain on my muscles, to tear the muscle fibers so that they can repair and grow bigger. The body won't become stronger all by itself. Munching a chocolate bar and sitting on a park bench may be enjoyable, but it will not improve physical strength. Physical strength only comes through pain, hence the phrase, "no pain, no gain."

It is the same emotionally and spiritually. I won't grow, apart from pain. Thank God there are rests in the midst of pain when I can process what is going on and see the growth. But also, thank God for the suffering. I am a more mature man than I was fifteen years ago. I have learned to be content with less, to endure longer, to whine less often, to care for others who are suffering, and to know God's strength and presence. Can I grow, apart from suffering? I'm not sure. Maybe I can. But what I am sure of, is that I would not have experienced the growth I just mentioned apart from the suffering God has allowed in my life. Suffering is the price of admission to live the life of the person I've always wanted to be.

AUTHENTICITY

Five times I received from the Jews the forty lashes minus one. Three times I was beaten with rods, once I was stoned, three times I was shipwrecked, I spent a night and a day in the open sea, I have been constantly on the move. I have been in danger from rivers, in danger from bandits, in danger from my own countrymen, in danger from Gentiles; in danger in the city, in danger in the country, in danger at sea; and in danger from false brothers. I have labored and toiled and have often gone without sleep; I have known hunger and thirst and have often gone without food; I have been cold and naked. (2 Corinthians 11:24-27)

Have you ever had a person give you advice about how to handle your difficult situation and you know they have no clue what you are going through? They speak in platitudes and banal declarations; you can almost lip sync their opinions because they are so prescribed and rehearsed. Compare that to someone who has experienced some of the exact same things you are struggling with. That person's advice (if given at all) is sensitive and understanding. They offer a view from experience and it rings true in your ears. You have camaraderie with them; they have earned the right to speak.

In Peter Jackson's 2002 version of the The Lord of the Rings: The Two Towers, there is an epic battle scene that takes place at Helm's Deep. It took Jackson the same amount of time to shoot that one battle scene that most producers would take to shoot an entire movie. The work was grueling, with most of the filming taking place at night in the cold, incessant rain. At the end of it, the actors and crew all got tattoos as a symbol and reminder that they had survived the epic event. They had overcome a huge obstacle together and had earned the right to be able to say, "I was there." They could understand and relate to their fellow actors who were having a hard time of it during the filming. For one of them to say to their comrades, "Keep going, don't give up" meant a lot more than for someone on the outside to say the same words.

There is something powerful in being able to say, "I was there" in regards to the suffering and difficulties of life. Suffering is all around me and if I want to be able to speak hope into others' lives, my own suffering will open that door.

On another note, this is why we can so fully trust the Lord Jesus Christ; He was "there" in suffering as well.

For we do not have a high priest who is unable to sympathize with our weaknesses, but we have one who has been tempted in every way, just as we are—yet was without sin. (Hebrews 4:15)

He understands suffering. He has been there. He is able to speak from authentic experience and encourage me, not from a distance, but up close and personal.

The Parable of the Lighthouse

Once there was a stalwart lighthouse that stood tall and proud on the shores of Nova Scotia, Canada, looking out towards the mighty Atlantic Ocean. For years it had weathered heavy storms, and the pounding of the waves as they broke over it had left its walls battered and worn. Though each portent of black cloud brought a wave of dismay over the lighthouse, it endured and shone its light proudly out over the dark waters.

It lived a very different life than its cousin, the gazebo, which resided in the central park of the nearby village. Oh sure, the gazebo had to endure the onslaught of nature too, but the town in which it resided was nestled in a low valley and the surrounding hills protected it from the full weight of nature's force.

One day, the gazebo got to talking with his fellow buildings.

"My poor cousin, the lighthouse. She stands out there by the ocean, having to endure the worst conditions one can imagine. We must do something for her."

All the other buildings agreed and with a concerted effort, they were able to relocate the lighthouse right next to the gazebo.

"Now, isn't this better?" asked the gazebo.

"Why yes, it truly is," answered the lighthouse, gazing around wondrously at her new environment.

"You will be safe now from the storms," the gazebo said. "Just wait till the first one comes. You won't believe how much cozier we are in here."

The lighthouse didn't have to wait long to find out. Barely three days later, a mighty nor'easter swept over the ocean, pounding the coastline with angry waves. The blackened sky spewed rain in great and unending torrents. The wind roared and howled as lightning and thunder filled the air. In the little village, the gazebo called out in elation to the lighthouse.

"Isn't it just as I told you? We only feel the rain and the small effects of the wind."

The lighthouse agreed but didn't appear to be very happy.

"What's the matter?" asked the gazebo. "Don't you feel more at ease here?"

"Why yes, of course," answered the lighthouse.

"Then why do you appear so troubled?"

"I am worried about the ships."

"What ships?"

"The ships that sail on the angry ocean. They depend on me to lead them safely home. If they can't see my light, they will be dashed on the rocks."

"Can't you lead them home from the safety of our village?"

"I wish I could, but I see now that the only way I can be of help to those desperate suffering ships, is for me to stand in the storm."

"But that won't be pleasant for you."

"No it won't, but it will produce a great work. It is what I was meant for."

As soon as she came to that conclusion, she picked herself up and hurried back to her place by the sea, defiant and determined in the face of the storm.

CHAPTER 6

WHAT ABOUT HEALING?

I knew a man who had only been a follower of Jesus for a few years. He was married and his wife was pregnant with their second child. When the child was born, it was obvious that something was wrong. The little boy's spine was twisted; one leg was shorter than the other and he couldn't turn his head to the right. The man didn't know what to do. An operation was going to cost more than the man could afford. Every morning, he would lay the small child on the kitchen table and pray for him.

"Dear Lord, please heal my son."

It was a simple prayer; he had a simple faith. This went on morning after morning, cry after cry. Then, one early spring morning, while the man sipped his coffee and prayed for his son, something extraordinary happened. The little baby turned his head to look at his dad. At first it didn't register with the humble man, but then it hit him: the child's head had turned to the right. With great elation and cautious excitement, the man checked his son over only to discover that what he had been praying for was granted. The boy's legs were the same length and his little spine was no longer twisted.

What an incredible gift that was for that man. What an incredible gift for that little boy. His life was made drastically different because of that one miraculous act of healing. I know this to be true, because I was that little baby lying on the table.

I know Christ can heal; I am living proof, but I also know that often people are not healed.

Fast forward thirty-five years. That same man is still following Jesus. His faith has become a masterpiece of depth and beauty. He has been transformed to look more and more like the Savior he serves. Then one day, he discovers that he has asbestos cancer. He is only sixty years old.

Now I am in the place of praying for him. I and many, many others bring the request for God's healing touch on dad. He's still so young. He has spent almost four decades humbly seeking after God. His life touched the lives of many others.

"Dear Lord, please heal my dad."

It was a simple prayer; I have a simple faith.

God did not heal my dad. He died thirteen months after being diagnosed.

This is the pattern I see when it comes to healing and God, or rather, this is the lack of pattern I see. His healing seems so random.

In Mark 4, a woman had been suffering with illness for twelve years. She had spent all her money on doctors, but instead of getting better she grew worse. When she heard that Jesus had come to town, she pushed forward through the crowd of people that surrounded Him. Coming up behind Him in the crowd, she reached out and touched His cloak because she figured that if she could just touch Him, she would be healed. And guess what? She was healed. Immediately after touching him, her suffering stopped and she could actually feel in her body that she had been freed from her suffering. There was a huge crowd pressing against Jesus as well, but only she was healed.

So, I ask, why her? Why was she the only one in that crowd who was healed? Was it because her suffering was the greatest of all the suffering in the crowd? She had been bleeding for twelve years. That is significant suffering to be sure, but at least there was a time in her life when she wasn't bleeding. What about someone born blind? Wouldn't their suffering be at least as bad as hers? The Bible says she had spent all her money on doctors, but doesn't that imply that at one time she had money? What about the many who were born into poverty, who never knew what it was like to have money? Surely, their cause was greater. Maybe it was because she had greater faith than everyone else. After all, she came forward to touch His cloak, believing that if she touched Him she would be healed. But what was everyone else doing that day? They were all pushing and pressing around Him. Why were they doing that? A couple of verses earlier it explains why the crowds were pressing around him. *"Because He had healed many so that those with various diseases were pushing forward to touch Him."* The woman wasn't alone in her risky venture of faith, so why was she the only one to get healed?

Here is the only answer I can come up with: some get healed and some don't.

This is terribly confusing, and potentially quite hurtful. When I visited Cave Church in Cairo, I passed by a room that was filled with wheel chairs, crutches and canes. These were all the cast off and no longer needed implements of people who had been healed. That was impressive, but I also knew that thousands and thousands of people attended that church, people who were poor and without adequate medical care and there weren't thousands and thousands of wheel chairs in that room.

Some get healed and some don't.

Isaiah says, *"But he was pierced for our transgressions, He was crushed for our iniquities; the punishment that brought us peace was upon Him, and by His wounds we are healed"* (Isaiah 53:6).

So are we healed or aren't we?

I wish it was a simple, provable fact. I have thought about this a lot, and I have a lot of questions. Many people are constantly praying for my healing. I have been anointed with oil and prayed for by my elders. I have confessed my sins and I believe that Jesus can heal (after all, He's done it for me before). But I am not healed. Maybe I am only allowed one healing in my life? Why couldn't that be enough? Does God owe me more? Do I have some kind of coupon book with five "get out of sickness free" cards? And why didn't my dad even get one?

Here are my few and meager thoughts about healing.

First, healing is a gift from God. I can't demand a gift, otherwise it is no longer a gift, but an obligation. I can't expect a gift either or the same is true. Healing is just one of the many gifts that God has given me. If I complain that He has not given me the gift I want, and ignore all the other gifts I have received, what does that say about me? Love is not about getting something from someone. Love is about "the someone"…period.

Second, every physical healing, no matter what it is, has a shelf life. By that I mean that we are all going to die. Isn't death the ultimate slap in the face of physical healing? If Jesus really did heal all those holy people who humbly asked, wouldn't there be even a few 600 year old saints walking around? God healed Job, a man filled with pains and sores. But one day, sometime after that healing, Job's body broke down again, and that time there was no healing. Jesus raised his friend Lazarus from the dead. This is an incredible story. The reality though, is that Lazarus had to suffer and die a second time.

Third, how do I know that God hasn't healed me? Oh sure, maybe He hasn't healed me of my stress and anxiety disorder, and maybe my kidney function isn't getting any better, but does that mean He hasn't healed me? I would never have known about the healing I received as an infant had my dad not told me that story; I could just as easily have been healed and remained ignorant about it my whole life. I would then be mistaken if I said that I had never been healed. Maybe there are all kinds of physical healings that I am unaware of. It's not beyond the scope of possibility.

I was diagnosed with severe sleep apnea with upwards of ninety episodes an hour. This meant that over seven hundred times a night, my heart would stop beating and I would gasp for breath. The clinician who finally diagnosed me said that it was one of the worst cases she had ever seen and she was amazed that I hadn't had a stroke or a heart attack. Can I give God healing credit for that? I believe I can, and I do.

Fourth, what is broken in me that needs healing? Of course I could make a quick list of my health issues: renal failure, hernia, high blood pressure, anxiety and stress disorder, gout, reactive arthritis. But that is not all that is broken in me. I am broken and sick spiritually. I have a faith that is weak and immature. I have an understanding of God that is skewed by my mortal perceptions and circumstances. I am broken mentally. I am filled with incorrect ideas and perceptions of who I am and how I function best in society. I am overly dependent on the praise of people. I still feel that I need to do stuff to be significant. I chase after things that won't last and neglect the things that are eternal. I am broken.

Here's the amazing news about that other brokenness: Christ is healing me of those things. I am becoming less of a people pleaser. I am trusting more in God. At first I complained loudly after only a couple of days of suffering, now I can go almost a year before I give in to my immature despair and lack of faith. Maybe one day, it will be five years before I start to question God. He is healing me! He has always been healing me.

And here's an even bigger kicker: God uses physical brokenness to achieve healing in the other realms. He allows brokenness in the temporal things to produce healing in the eternal things. That's good business if you ask me.

There is more to gain by not healing than by healing. Therefore, it seems to me that the kindest thing God could ever do for me is not to relieve my suffering, but rather to be with me in it.

Should I pray for healing then? Absolutely!

CHAPTER 7

GIVE THE COMMAND TO SAVE ME

I have been dreading this chapter because I know it is going to expose a particular spiritual struggle that I wish I didn't have. I have a hard time with prayer.

When I was 14, I began a disciplined spiritual life of going for a walk for a half hour every morning to pray and then coming home and reading the Bible for a half hour. Did it ever get legalistic? I'm sure there were strong hints of legalism in there, but my motives were truly just to be closer to God.

My prayers consisted of lists of rotating items that I would cover on a regular basis. It would look something like this:

On Monday, I would pray for my mom, for school, for the little kid I sponsored through World Vision and for my youth group.

On Tuesday, I would pray for my dad, my buddies at school, for the girl I was going to marry, for a missionary and for my pastor

On Wednesday, I'd pray for my older brother, Mike, for my grades, for an unsaved friend...

Well, you get the idea. I was very faithful and very consistent. And it all felt quite rote. I did this for many years though, changing the lists every few months as needs arose. Some things remained constant, like having my parents and my siblings on it. Some things were added, like my wife and then my kids as they came along. But at some point, I just began to question the whole process.

Why was I praying for those things over and over again? Couldn't I just tape the list to the top of my head and let God read it Himself?

I began to wonder what was actually going on when I prayed and asked for things. Was it something like this?

Me: Dear Lord, please help that man in the church who lost his job. Help him take care of His family.

Pseudo-God: You know, I never even thought about that. Great suggestion Tim! Ya, I really should do something about that guy.

I began to think of how desperate the situation was if God was only going to do things in response to my prayers. I am mostly self-centered and often oblivious to the needs of people around me. If they were going to be stuck in their suffering simply because I didn't formulate the words to put God in play, they were in for a long, hard road.

Then someone tried to enlighten me. They said, "When you pray, it is more about God changing you." I think they meant that when I pray for that guy in my church who lost his job, maybe God will inspire me to give some money to him. So, doesn't it follow then I could bypass prayer altogether and just match the needs I see with things I could do to help fill them?

I had a hard time justifying asking for things in prayer. Jesus said, in the Sermon on the Mount, *"Your heavenly Father knows what you need before you ask Him."* Wouldn't it be more Godly, more trusting, more mature to say, "God you know my needs, I believe that you will do what you think is best in my life. I trust all that I have as your provision for me"?

Why spend time asking for things God already knows I need? Am I just reminding Him of His job as though maybe He had a lapse in concentration?

I have no trouble in thanking God in prayer and praising Him. Those things seem to make more sense to me. I believe that prayer is a conversation, and by nature should be two-way. And in that conversation, I have grown tired of hearing me talk all the time. I want to hear God talk more. It makes sense that if one of us should have the microphone more, it should be God. One of the reasons I memorize and rehearse scripture so often is so that I can hear God's voice. By saying the scriptures over and over in my head, I am giving Him the greatest opportunity to speak to me.

And yet, my position on not asking for things in prayer doesn't jibe with the scriptures that I am memorizing.

Paul says in Colossians, *"We have not stopped praying for you."* And later, *"Pray for us, too."*

David writes: *"Give ear to my words, O LORD, consider my sighing. Listen to my cry for help, my King and my God, for to you I pray. In the morning, O LORD, you hear my voice; in the morning I lay my requests before you and wait in expectation."* *(Psalm 5:1-3)*

Jonah says, *"In my despair, I called to the Lord and He heard my cry."*

And Jesus clearly says, *"Ask and it will be given to you...for whoever asks receives."* *(Matthew 7:7 & 8)*

It seems pretty clear that we are supposed to pray and ask.

So what should I pray for, and what can I expect when I pray? Is it okay to pray for things I want? Is there an approved list of prayer requests that I can choose from? In the last year, one verse has done more to shape my concept of prayer requests than any other.

In John 15:7, Jesus said, *"If you remain in me and my words remain in you, ask whatever you wish, and it will be given you."*

At first, this verse seemed particularly troubling to me. It bothered me that Jesus would say such a thing. Here's how I would have rephrased it (I'm sure God gets these kinds of editorial suggestions all the time).

*"If you remain in me and my words remain in you, ask whatever you wish **and I will give you only the things on your list that I want to.**"*

This would make sense. I could accept this. But He seems to say that I can ask for anything and He will give it to me.

Or how about this: *"If you **could** remain in me and my words **did really** remain in you, you **could** ask for anything you wish and it will be given you **(but we both know that isn't likely to happen)**."*

It's like holding a cookie too high up over a two-year old and saying, "Sure you can have this cookie; all you have to do is jump up and grab it."

Honestly, the verse made me mad. So, I decided to put it to the test. I just started asking for anything I wished for. I wished for $53,000 (I know, a strange number, but it was my wish). I wished that my kidneys were better. I wished that my books would sell. I wished that I could go back to work. In my frustration with trying to figure out this whole prayer thing, I was at least going to show God the folly of His words. This was honestly the best thing I could have done. Instead of trying to make excuses for God's apparent lack of honesty, I was going to force Him to face it. And in His kindness, He brought me to a very important discovery.

The Wish Hierarchy Principle

> *Me: God, didn't you say that I could ask for anything I wish and you would give it to me?*
> *God: Um...something like that...*
> *Me: I wish I could be done with this suffering.*
> *God: What else do you wish for?*
> *Me: I wish I was a stronger man.*
> *God: Which do you wish for more?*

What do I wish for more?

Let's say I am buying something from a convenience store. When I go to make my purchase, the cashier foolishly steps away from the counter for a moment leaving the cash register open. Immediately I have two wishes:

Wish One: I wish I had that free money sitting there.
Wish Two: I wish to be an honest man.

I can't have both of those wishes; they are mutually exclusive. Suddenly, I am faced with a hierarchy of wishes. Will my wish to take the money be greater than my wish to be honest? Or will my wish to be honest outweigh my wish to be a thief.

Let's say I am on a business trip away from my wife and a beautiful young woman starts showing interest in me. Again, I am faced with two wishes. Will I follow the wish to engage in exciting and enticing activity, or will I follow my wish to be a faithful and loving husband?

When Jesus tells me to ask for anything I wish, He is allowing me to honestly evaluate my hierarchy of wishes. Now, He doesn't do this blindly; He wants to help me make the best use of this freedom, so He sets a couple of ground rules. "Remain in Me," He says. "Let My words remain in you." It is only as this happens that I can be sure of what to wish for.

But this is a bit of a sliding scale. How do I know I am remaining in Him and His words are remaining in me? I will never do this perfectly or consistently; some days will be better than others.

The answer: God understands this dilemma and He beckons me to ask anyway. So I ask, and in the process of my asking, if I am humble and listening to God, remaining in Him in the midst of my disappointment and confusion, He aids me in ordering my hierarchy correctly.

So, I ask for $53,000 (seriously, I really did). God heard me. He placed the request on the table between us and asked, "Is there any other money related wish that you have?" It took a bit of effort to force my attention away from the fifty-three grand, but once I did, there was actually another request that I had. I wished that I could live a life of contentment. In my confusion, I had associated the two requests as one; if I had $53,000 I would be content. But actually, they were two separate items. I have met people who have that extra $53,000. I have even met some who have had an extra $530,000 or $5,300,000 and have discovered that they weren't content.

Now there were two wishes on the table: on the one side $53,000 and, on the other side, contentment. Quietly, God prodded me with a final question, "Which do you wish for more?" Were the two requests mutually exclusive? It's possible, and in my case it was certain. I was able to see clearly into the desires of my heart (albeit on this one tiny issue only). Looking back into the eyes of my Heavenly Father I responded, "More than anything, I wish I was content." A smile broke out on His face. "Done," He said.   This is my new process for asking things in prayer. I ask for whatever I wish. I ask it humbly and with my eyes wide open. I compare the wishes and rank them as best as I can and I trust that God will help me make sense of things.

Jesus, Himself, models this hierarchy of wishes. In the garden of Gethsemane, on the night He was betrayed, He offered up His wishes to His Father. "Please take this cup of suffering away from Me. I desperately wish that I wouldn't have to go through the pain and horror of these next days." This was His passionate wish. In fact, His tears fell like drops of blood. But He also had another wish. "I want Your will to be done, Father. Your will, first and foremost in everything." And in His system of hierarchy, it was the second wish that was greater than the first.

Almost daily, I ask God to allow me to go back to work. I also ask that His perfect intent will be done in my life and that I will patiently trust His timing. It is the second wish that has priority over the first. I still ask the first, I want the first, but I also want the second and if I cannot have both, I want the second more.

In James 5 we are told to come and ask for prayer for healing. I have done this, both for myself and for others, and I will continue to do this until the day I die. But I also know that God may be answering a greater wish of mine, even if I don't know that I have it yet. So, my prayers are always infused with a humble awareness of my limited understanding.

CHAPTER 8

THIS BEAUTIFUL LAND

"The Lord is my shepherd, I shall not want. He makes me lie down in green pastures." (Psalm 23:1)

I have always loved Psalm 23. It was one of the first ones I memorized as a young boy. My dad would have the words up on the fridge, and if we learned them we got prizes. In those days, I couldn't imagine any other benefit to learning those verses than the prizes; come on, what could be better than a cool twenty-five cents? Over the years, I have gleaned unfathomable benefit from God's Word in my life. Psalm 23 is one of those examples.

This Psalm is often read at funerals because of its hope of heaven as well as its promise of comfort during times of darkness and suffering. It also paints a lovely picture of a contented sheep being fully taken care of by the shepherd. The line that has impacted me so much in the last several years is the one that says, "He makes me lie down." It doesn't say that I lie down on my own or that He invites me to rest. No, He *makes* me lie down. For some reason I won't lie down on my own accord. I will go and go and go, pushing myself at a frenetic pace, not stopping to assess my life or my relationships. So, the Shepherd, who knows and loves me deeply, makes me lie down.

It is in this lying down that I have time.

Time to think and reflect.

Time to evaluate and grade.

Time to wonder and dream.

Time to listen.

Time to love.

I have shown by my lifestyle that I won't lie down, I won't take the time necessary to do healthy soul maintenance. God, in His mercy, allows suffering to make me stop.

At first, I hate this place. I want to be through it as quickly as possible. I want to be back working and running and "living". At first, there is nothing about this place that interests me. At first, this place feels more like a dank, gray jail than a lush, green pasture. But when that initial reaction wears off (and it can take anywhere from a day to a year) I begin to look around and see that this pasture is actually quite a lovely place. There are certain aspects of this land that are particularly lovely.

The first is a shedding of illusion. I am amazed at the madness in which I live a lot of the time. I live like I can foretell the future and I have control of my destiny. Even as I write this, a good friend of mine is sitting in the hospital. On his way to work yesterday, a semi-truck lost control and slammed into his pickup head on. It could have killed him. Instead my friend sits in a hospital room with multiple broken bones and a newer understanding of how quickly everything can change. I have another friend whose 23 year-old son got married two weeks ago. Two days ago, the son fell down an elevator shaft at work and was killed. The horror and pain of that situation is beyond description. How do you make sense out of that? One thing we do know is that young man was not planning on dying when he kissed his new bride good-bye that day.

We have no idea what the future will hold. James says, *"Now listen, you who say, 'Today or tomorrow we will go to this or that city, spend a year there, carry on business and make*

money.' Why, you do not even know what will happen tomorrow.
What is your life? You are a mist that appears for a little while
and then vanishes." (James 4). Suffering brings my mortality
into stark relief. I am forced to realize that I am frail, made of
dust and on the inevitable road of returning to dust.

I also live like possessions matter, as though things make
up the essence of my life. When suffering comes, and those
things are stripped away, I get to see through the illusion and
realize that none of it really counts for much. Fame and
significance become less important. Promotion and importance
begin to fade. What matters is who I am and who I love.

A second beautiful characteristic of this green pasture in
which I have been made to lie down is that I am forced to live day
to day. I find that I appreciate little things more, things I normally
take for granted. I love the days when I am not in pain. I am so
grateful that I have a house where I can live safely with my wife
and children. I am so thankful for the food that is on the table
before us. I love every opportunity I get to make a difference in
another person's life. I love it when I can share a meaningful
conversation with a friend over coffee or over the phone or
through social media. These things are always precious, but when
I am at peak health I often do not take the time to appreciate
them; it almost seems that their perceived value is inversely
proportional to how fast I am going.

I had a friend who spent some time in Africa as a
missionary. She went there armed with her passion to serve, and
her North American "get it done" mentality. One of the things
that drove her crazy was the time that the African women in the
village would spend "doing nothing" but sitting and visiting. She
often felt like she was the only one getting anything of

significance done. Near the end of her time there, one of the women said to her in a kind and concerned voice, "You Canadians are always so busy, but you are never getting anything done." Her busyness was forcing her to miss out on the most important experiences of this life: our relationships.

When I live day to day, I am more apt to look for what is most important.

The final benefit to this beautiful land is the closeness I experience with God. The shepherd does not make the sheep lie down in a green pasture and then leave them there. He stays with the sheep. It's quiet there and his voice can be heard.

I went to a retreat recently and was led through a self-assessment exercise. It was in the form of a simple questionnaire, and asked questions like:

-Am I able to take time for my health?
-Do I find that my family relationships are healthy   and well cared for?
-Do I feel rested and refreshed?
-Do I feel close to God and are my spiritual   disciplines being attended to?

I was to measure myself on a sliding scale from "this is mostly true" to "this is never true." I had done this kind of questionnaire in the past and often my scores hovered near the 'never true' end of the spectrum. I wasn't exercising. My family was going in a million different directions and I was leading the charge. I felt exhausted and on the verge of burnout and my time with God was thin and utilitarian. I was surprised then when I filled out the questionnaire this time; it was completely opposite.

Nowadays, all I seem to do is monitor and guard my health. My familial relationships have their normal difficulties, but I have the time and availability to work through those difficulties. Consequently, we are as close as we have ever been. I am far away from feelings of burnout. Most importantly, however, I am able to be close to God and feel His presence close to me.

Being close to my Creator is the most important thing in my life. Since He created me, and since He knows everything about me, and His understanding of reality and time is infinite, the very best place for me to be is close to His heart. There are so many messages being blasted at me, so many labels pinned to my lapel (most of which are untrue). I need a place to go, away from the noise and the madness of this world, to hear what is really true. But, so often I am part of the madness and won't slow down long enough to listen.

In the past, I filled out the questionnaire with trepidation and no small amount of guilt. I used to long for the kind of assessment that I got this last time through. Suddenly, it hit me; I was living the dream. I had the old way of life painfully stripped away from me, the old way that was keeping me from being the kind of person that I had always wanted to be, and what I was left with was an unwanted, unlooked for reality that produced in me the qualities that I had most been longing for.

It made me wonder, "When is it that I am *really* sick?"

Am I most healthy when I am not paying attention to the things that really matter, when I rush past my kids without taking the time to notice them, when I believe the lie that I will live forever, when I attribute more value to a paycheck than a relationship? Currently my body isn't doing so well, but my soul is better than it has ever been.

I love this place, the pasture in which I have been forced to lie down. I love the feeling of peace that is here. I love the gentle play of the wind over the grass. I love the camaraderie of my fellow flock members who, like me, have been made to lie down. I love the care and intentionality of the Shepherd who acts sometimes contrary to my will, but always for my benefit.

It is a simple place. It is a place of honesty and truth. It is a place of rest. I don't know if I am going to get better. I hope I am. I am planning on it. But the thing that worries me the most is leaving this quiet pasture. Is it possible to go back into the realities of life outside of suffering and still maintain the quietness of the green pasture? I hope and pray that it is so.

CHAPTER 9

TOOLS OF THE TRADE

I golf. I'm not that great, but I sure do love it. I usually shoot 18 over or bogey golf. According to the USGA, I am slightly worse than average (the average handicap for men is 16.1). Nonetheless, if I have the time and money, one of my favorite things is an early morning round on perfectly manicured fairways and greens. I have a few clubs in my bag that are my favorites; they just feel better than the rest. I can hit them consistently and feel very confident whenever they are in my hands. However, despite the preference for those few clubs, I would be foolish if I only brought those ones with me on the course. During a round of golf, though I use my favorite clubs the most, I use almost every other club in my bag at some point or other. The better I am able to hit those other clubs, the better my score will be.

This is similar to my approach in handling suffering. We most often don't get to choose whether or not we will suffer, but we always get to choose our attitudes and responses towards the suffering we experience. There are several attitudes that I have tried to adopt in my quest to learn to deal with the suffering I experience. Some of them feel more natural than others, like my favorite golf clubs. Others I mis-hit so badly that I can end up several fairways away from my destination. I suppose it might be fair to say that I am a bogey sufferer. But God is slowly helping me to develop these attitudes, and over time, maybe I will be somewhat better than "worse than average" in how I handle suffering. Here are the tools that have most effectively helped me in my suffering.

HONESTY

I have six children. That has made life both incredibly difficult and unimaginably wonderful. I have learned much about my relationship with my Heavenly Father by observing and experiencing my relationships with my kids. One reassuring lesson I have learned is that I know more than my kids think I know.

One day, I came upon one of my sons, who was four years old at the time. I noticed right away that he had an obviously guilty look on his face and his hands were hidden behind his back. A quick glance around the room revealed the sugar bowl lid sitting on the counter.

"So, what's going on?" I asked.

"Nothing," he replied.

"Really? There's nothing you're hiding from me?"

"No."

"Can I see your hands?"

It wasn't until that moment that he realized he had been found out. He had been eating sugar straight from the bowl and, in his mind, had been doing a decent job bluffing me.

I seem to often think I can respond this way to God. Suffering comes my way and I have a real difficult time with it. I doubt His love for me. I am hurt and confused and disillusioned. But for some reason, I want to hide those feelings from God. I am so desirous to handle suffering well, that I mistakenly think I can bluff God by keeping my true feelings hidden. So, I put them behind my back and put on a brave face towards God.

Well, guess what? He knows. In fact, He knows the depth of my confusion and despair even better than I do.

God: How are you doing?

Me (lying): Fine. Super. Couldn't be better.

God (smiling): Really? Can I see your heart?

When He asks that, it isn't as though He doesn't know what is in my heart already. His question is more along the lines of, "Let's both look at the condition of your heart together."

It is only as I join God in honestly facing my real feelings and doubts, that I can begin to work through them. He knows that I am having a hard time trying to make sense of everything. He knows that I am questioning His love for me. And He is not overly bothered by those very real human responses that I am experiencing. But He wants to help me work it through. He wants to process it with me.

EXPECTANCY

Another tool of the trade is expectancy.

My dear wife has spent four and a half years of her life pregnant. Imagine that. Fifty-four months of being with child. That's a long time to be carrying babies. However, I must say, she made pregnancy look beautiful and, for the most part, she actually loved it. During those months, like many other parents-to-be, we said we were expecting. We were expecting something, or rather someone, wonderful to be coming soon. But labor and delivery were never a walk in the park. I can remember being in tears and awe at the amount of pain my amazing wife had to endure to bring each of our kids into this world. But she was willing to do it because of the reward at the end. When the pain was finally over and the precious child was cradled in her arms, she was exhausted, but overjoyed.

Paul says, *"I consider that our present sufferings are not worth comparing with the glory that will be revealed in us."* *(Romans 8:18)*

God is doing a good work in me. He is redeeming the dark road of suffering and creating in me something of great value. I think that while the "glory that will be revealed in us" finds its ultimate fulfillment in heaven, there is much glory that is revealed here on earth as well. Consequently, when I suffer, I want to look at it with the eyes of expectation. I am expecting. God is working in me. I will be different than I was before the suffering.

ACCEPTANCE

For many years, my family reunion has taken place in Revelstoke, British Columbia. It is a picturesque little town along the Columbia River, nestled amongst mighty mountains. In the winter, it is a destination for skiers, snowboarders and skidoo-ers. In the summer, it offers great fishing, hiking, mountain-biking and skateboarding. Every year, most of my siblings and our spouses and children make the 14 km round trip hike into Eva Lake from the top of Mount Revelstoke. It is a beautiful hike through meadows lush with mountain flowers and the scent of pine permeating the cool mountain air. I always come to the end of that hike very pleased that we chose to do it again. However, I also come to the end of that hike somewhat tired and sore. My pain from the hike is in exact proportion to the degree of my lack of exercise before the reunion. Yet, exercise or no, I still go on the hike; I just accept that I am going to feel pain afterwards.

We have the amazing opportunity to live one life here on planet earth. It is a life of wonder and adventure and discovery. It is a life with hilarious laughter, passionate love, and thrilling challenge. But part of this life is also pain and suffering. It's just the way it is. If I am of the mindset that I shouldn't suffer, I will be shocked and disappointed. But if I accept suffering as just part of this fantastic privilege called life, it can put me in a better frame of mind. Of course, this mindset doesn't make the suffering go away, but it does keep me from adding more negative layers to sift through. By accepting suffering as a necessary part of life, I am not saying that I shouldn't try to prevent suffering in my life. Life is filled with war and poverty and injustice; I need to do my part to fight against those things, and I would be naïve to think that I shouldn't be touched by them.

TEACHABILITY

Do you want to know what separates a Chess Grand Master from a good chess player? The Grand Master has experienced a lot more loss. They have played a lot more games, have won a lot more games and have lost a lot more games. And it is in the replaying and studying of those losses, with a teachable mind, that a good chess player becomes a great chess player.

This is true with acting or plumbing or inventing or writing. It is true with everything that matters in this life. Some say that we learn by failure. I believe this is only partly true. At times, I have the uncanny ability to remain ignorant despite my failure. I must fail, yes, but I must also have eyes to see and ears to hear. My heart and mind must be open to learn through the experience, to see what wisdom can be gleaned from it, and to be willing to do whatever I can to make changes.

I am terrible at video games; I die quickly in every game I play. I watch my son Riise play, and am astounded at how good he is. My explanation for the vast difference in our skill levels is that when his player dies, he makes note of how and why it happens. He learns from it and avoids some of the same disasters as he progresses through the game. Does that mean he never dies anymore? Of course not. The game keeps getting more and more challenging, but his understanding and knowledge also grow, and he has experienced much more of the joy and entertainment the game was meant to provide than I will ever know.

He has a teachable spirit. When I simply get hurt and angry with the suffering that I experience, I only receive the devastation of that suffering. But when I have a teachable spirit and humbly look for what I can learn through the suffering, I gain so much more.

COURAGE

A fifth tool of the trade is courage.

My buddy Rob is one of the most courageous people I know. When he was in his twenties, he opted to leave behind the privileges and comforts of his upbringing to move into a low-income, high crime area of our city. He did this because he wanted to more effectively show love and kindness to high risk kids.

Rob also has a heart for the poor and homeless. He is often serving them through some of the great organizations in our city set up for that purpose. But serving wasn't enough. He wanted to associate deeper with them. So, with five dollars in his pocket, he decided to go and be homeless for a week (he gave away the five dollars after the first hour). He begged on the streets, slept in the shelters, ate whatever he could find. He had no safety net, no warm vehicle to hide out in when the temperature dropped.

I have often remarked to him that he is one of the most courageous people I know. I still remember something he said once. "Courage is not the lack of fear, rather it is the determination to do something, despite the fear." I had assumed that he was just "less scared" than I was, but he would say that he was just more determined to not let fear stop him from doing what he knew was right.

His answer rang true to me. Maybe because I had seen it in another man I deeply respect.

On the night before He was betrayed, Jesus cried out in the garden of Gethsemane for His Father to take away the terror of the next few days. "If there is any way that this cup can be taken from me, please do so," He begged. He was truly dreading the suffering about to come, but He also expressed supreme courage by making His next request. "But not my will, but Yours be done." He was determined that despite the horror of what He was about to endure, He would face it nonetheless.

I want to have this attitude with every instance of suffering that comes my way. I want to face it with fortitude and determination. I don't want it to have so much power over me that I cower in trepidation. God is at my side, whom shall I fear?

ENDURANCE

My son Luke played three years of hockey. He mostly played defense, and right from the beginning he was a leader on his team. There were other players with more skill, but he had a natural ability to encourage and bring his teammates together.

The first two years were pure hockey bliss. They had their share of losses, but overall his teams experienced winning seasons. Both years, Luke's team won the championship. He loved hockey in those years. He couldn't wait until the next game when his team could trounce their opponents. Then came Luke's final year. There was a major reshuffling of the teams and Luke found that he was no longer with his friends of the past two years. Still, with optimistic hope in his heart, he dove into the new season. They lost their first game. Badly. It was a wake up call, as he quickly began to assess both his own skills and the collective skills of his new team.

"It's just the first game," I said. "You guys will settle down and figure each other out better as the season progresses."

They lost their second game. And their third. And their fourth through tenth. Then their eleventh through twentieth. It was a very long season. My pithy little statements disappeared like scratches in the ice under the Zamboni. I went to game after game, wishing with all my heart that his team would win, only to walk away disappointed. But though I was disappointed in their record, I was growing in leaps and bounds in my respect for Luke. He endured.

It wasn't easy, and it would be a lie to say that he never wanted to quit, but he kept at it. He played every shift full out. He gave more of himself than he had in the previous two years combined. He scored more goals, broke up more plays, gave more encouragements to his goalie, and skated faster and faster. The kind of player he was at the end of the season was so much greater than when he started. And when they won their first game (I think it was game twenty-three), his team celebrated like Stanley Cup winners.

Sometimes I wonder whether most of life is simply about enduring. Helen Keller said, *"Character cannot be developed in ease and quiet. Only through experience of trial and suffering can the soul be strengthened, ambition inspired, and success achieved."*

Around the same time, Henry Ford said, *"Life is a series of experiences, each one of which makes us bigger, even though sometimes it is hard to realize this. For the world was built to develop character, and we must learn that the setbacks and grieves which we endure help us in our marching onward."*

If I just had a greater ability to endure, I wonder how much the rest would simply fall naturally in place.

HEAVENLY PERSPECTIVE

A final tool of the trade is having a heavenly perspective.

We used to live out in the country on a couple of acres. Almost one acre of that was lawn. At some point, we got a riding lawn mower and then Jennifer and I would fight over whose turn it was to mow the lawn. However, there was no fighting before the riding lawn mower. In the days of the push mower, when it took two hours to mow the lawn, I was given full reign of the responsibility. Actually, it wasn't really all that bad. I love mowing lawns. To me, it's another form of artistic expression. I love walking around after the job is done, appreciating the patterns I have "painted" in the grass with the mower.

The trick with a huge lawn is keeping the lines straight. To do this, you can't focus on the ground in front of you, you have to focus on a spot in the distance. I would select a tree in the adjoining forest and, keeping my attention on it, push the mower directly towards it. When I reached the edge of my lawn, I was rewarded by a straight line behind me.

Often I live my life looking at what is immediately around me. I see my current financial situation or my present health difficulties and I try to navigate as best I can emotionally with that limited perspective. It is no wonder that I am often lost and floundering.

When I focus on heaven, however, it changes how I live today. My time on this planet, whether it is 50 years or 90 years, is remarkably short compared to the span of eternity. There will come a day, thanks to the grace and kindness of God, when I will stand on the threshold of eternity in heaven. I imagine that in that moment I will look down the endless road of peace and joy that stretches out before me. Then, I will glance back at my life here on earth, a blip in comparison, and I will think, "Since this eternal joy is my future, I know I could have suffered more, and with a better attitude, during my life.

Paul says, *"For our light and momentary troubles are achieving for us an eternal glory that far outweighs them all." (2 Corinthians 4:17)*

Is Paul unaccustomed to real suffering? No, of course not. Rather, he has placed suffering up for comparison against eternity.

Recently, my garage door broke. I had to call in a serviceman to repair it, and it cost me just under three hundred dollars. That is no small amount of money. Jennifer and I just had to swallow that cost because we needed to get our vehicle out of our garage. Now, imagine that I had an original painting in the back of my truck that someone was willing to purchase for $100,000 if I could deliver it to them by noon. Suddenly, that $300 to get my garage door open would seem a paltry sum in comparison; it would be a light and momentary trouble.

I have very little ability to conceptualize eternity, which is why I must live by faith. I must choose to believe that whatever pain and sorrow I experience now, no matter how great or how extensive, will come to an end if my hope is in Christ. And it won't take many steps down that glorious road in heaven before the totality of my struggle here will fade away, forgotten.

CHAPTER 10

SO, WHAT DO I KNOW FOR SURE?

I am astounded at how small we really are in relation to all there is and how little we really know in relation to all that is knowable. The earth is just a tiny, infinitesimal speck randomly located in the universe. With what can I compare it? Imagine that I were to fly to Africa and walk five days out into the Sahara Desert until I could see nothing in any direction but sand dunes and sky. Then imagine that I grasped a handful of desert sand and let it sift through my fingers until only a few grains clung to my outstretched fingers. If I were to isolate one of those grains of sand and compare its size and location to the rest of the planet, it would be a similar comparison of our earth's size and location in relation to our Milky Way Galaxy. We are relatively miniscule.

There is so much that is beyond our ability to truly observe. What, for example, is on the other side of our own galaxy? There are theories that many scientists hold, but no one knows for certain because no one has ever actually seen the other side of our galaxy. When it comes to understanding the universe or the past or the future, so much of what is known is simply our best educated guess based on the currently available evidence.

Not only that, while we put a lot of stock into what we can see, I am astounded at how little we actually can see. Recently I was introduced to the mind-boggling facts of the Electromagnetic Spectrum, the entire spectrum of light including radio waves, microwaves, x-rays, gamma rays and visible light. How much of this spectrum can the human eye observe? Well, considering all that we can see, you might think that it is quite a wide range, but that's not so. If I were to take a garden hose (a very long garden hose) and stretch it out from Vancouver, British Columbia to the Manitoba-Ontario border, it would be approximately 3800km. If I were then to crimp the hose at, say, Regina, Saskatchewan, the width of that single fold line in comparison to the length of the hose would represent the proportion of the electromagnetic spectrum that the human eye can see. Everything else on the spectrum is invisible to us.

And as if that wasn't enough, even what I can see leaves me astounded. I can observe much, but understand little. For example, why does the male sea horse carry and give birth to the eggs? How do dandelions transform from yellow flower to white gossamer seed messengers? Why do I laugh or kiss or dream? The vastness and wonder of what I can observe around me is astonishing.

Solomon says, *"As you do not know the path of the wind or how a baby is formed in a mother's womb, so you cannot understand the work of God, the Maker of all things."* *(Ecclesiastes 11:5)*

I simply cannot fathom what God does, what He allows and disallows. The Bible teaches that His ways and thoughts are infinitely higher than my ways and thoughts; He thinks at an utterly deeper level than me. Case in point: in my limited vision and understanding of the world, I believe suffering should be eradicated from my life. Naturally, my first response to suffering is to cry out to God that I don't understand why the suffering is happening to me. But then I have the arrogance to get angry at God for seeing things differently, and I veer off course and say, "Because I don't understand, God, you must be in the wrong."

It would be like asking a three-year old from Alberta to grasp the subtleties of the Russian Ambassador's conversations with the Ambassador from China. It is conceivable that the three-year old could one day understand such an exchange (both ambassadors were three years old once themselves), but it would be a very small possibility. And this is only on the scale of humanity. When I pit my finite mind against the infinite mind of God, I have very little hope of understanding His grand scheme of things.

Compare just a couple of examples of God's work in the lives of two people in the Bible. The first is a man named Joseph. From the age of seventeen and on, he had a difficult road. He was first envied and rejected by his brothers, sold into slavery, falsely accused of sexual misconduct and jailed, and finally forgotten in an Egyptian prison. Yet the Bible says that God was with him through it all, and the end of the story is great. One day he is remembered and brought before Pharaoh. He impresses Pharaoh so much that the king makes Joseph the second-in-command over all of Egypt (and at that time, the whole world was looking to Egypt for their very survival). In effect, Joseph became the most powerful person in the world. That's a story that I can get behind. That's a God that makes a little more sense. Maybe I can understand the hardships of Joseph a little easier now that I have seen the end result.

But here's a second example. John the Baptist, Jesus' cousin, had, by all outward appearances, an incredibly successful ministry. Despite being dressed up in clothes made of camel's hair and living in the wilderness on a diet of locusts and wild honey, all the people from Jerusalem and from the Judean countryside came to him to be baptized. They left their homes to find him. Apparently, he was the main spiritual attraction. All the while, though, he was never confused by that fame. He constantly pointed people to the coming Messiah, and when Jesus eventually did show up on the scene, John graciously and humbly acknowledged Him as the greater One that was to come. But John wasn't done. The king, Herod, had married his own brother's wife, and John was declaring the act to be unlawful. He took a stand against the political corruption and ended up thrown in jail. I wonder if he pondered the story of Joseph during those days of incarceration. I wonder if when his disciples came and bemoaned his current situation, he encouraged them with Joseph's story.

Despite his unfair incarceration, John still had some solid tracks to run on. King Herod, whom John had been criticizing, was greatly puzzled whenever he heard John speak, but he liked to listen to him. Maybe this small grace was John's consolation. Maybe he said to his disciples, "I think I am suffering this injustice because it is giving me direct access to the king." Whatever John's attitude may have been, John's story doesn't end like Joseph's. One day, on Herod's birthday, the king gave a banquet for his key leaders. His step-daughter came in and danced and everyone was impressed. The king promised the girl anything she wanted. The girl asked her mother, Herod's illicit wife, what she should ask for. Her mother had been nursing a deep grudge against John for what he had been saying about her marriage. Without hesitation, she told her daughter to ask for John's head. The story quickly concludes after that. The girl asks for John's head and the king, concerned about his public image, complies. He complies! He sends an executioner to behead John in prison. That's it. John's life is over. That's not like Joseph's story at all. It doesn't seem to add up. John was a devoted follower and servant of God. Why wouldn't God redeem his situation like he redeemed Joseph's?

I don't know.

I have heard some people say that they don't want to follow God because he seems so capricious, and honestly, there have been times when I have felt that way too. But what are the alternatives? If seeming capriciousness is the deal–breaker to following God, what else could I put my trust in? The economy? The government? Myself?

I sometimes wonder if God's seemingly confusing manner is more like the classic example of the surprise birthday party. The birthday girl feels sad because no one seems to be remembering her birthday, when all the while her friends are planning something much greater. Though she thinks her friends don't care, they are actually filled with thoughts and plans of joy for her. Her disillusionment is based solely on the fact that she doesn't know everything there is to know about the situation.

And so I am faced with the stark truth that there is very little I know for sure. I am doing my best to make sense of my suffering, but sometimes suffering just doesn't make sense. At the end of it all, my conclusions are pretty simple.

1.   Life is filled with suffering; no one gets a free ride.

2.   One day this life will end, and then I will be with God in heaven where there will be   no more suffering.

3.   God promised that He would be with me in suffering.

This gives me the hope to go on, and so I continue to move forward through the suffering that comes my way. Sometimes I handle it well, often I handle it poorly. But either way, God is right there beside me helping me to face each challenge with His grace and strength and courage.

This also compels me to be an encouragement to others who suffer. Times of struggle and difficulty can be so dark that sometimes a person can see no way out. But there is a way through. Suffering does not have to be the final word.

I sincerely hope that in the few words I have written here, you have found some help in your journey of suffering. May God grant you His presence and strength in whatever circumstance you find yourself.

ONE FINAL WORD

I started writing this book five months ago. Since then, my kidney function has dropped significantly, I am still unable to work, and still have no clear idea what God has for me for the future. During the past five months there have been days here and there (and sometimes weeks here and there) where it has taken all my effort and energy to keep from giving into despair and hopelessness. Both my wife, Jennifer, and I have experienced these dark, dark times. But God has been with us through it all. And then, the other day, something extraordinary happened; I noticed that I was whistling.

Whistling!

I thought to myself, "How can I be whistling? I only whistle when I'm happy. I can only whistle when there is a song in my heart."

When I am sad or my heart is heavy, I don't have what it takes to whistle. This was truly amazing to me. I was quite surprised. I wasn't expecting it, but that is just how God works.

He gives supernatural peace when anxiety threatens to derail.

He gives supernatural joy when despair and sorrow flood over the edge.

And He gives supernatural hope when the future is completely unclear and threateningly bleak.

He promised that He would be with me in trouble and He has never let me down.

WHISPERS, GROANS AND PRAYERS
From the Book of Hope and Pain

In 2003, a very dear friend of mine lost his son in a motorcycle accident. The boy was only twelve years old. To say that it was a devastating experience would be an understatement of the greatest proportions. He and his wife asked me to come and officiate their son's funeral. As I flew from Calgary to Ontario, I was overwhelmed at the enormity of their grief and pain and I was at a loss as to what I could say that might bring comfort in any way.

I brought with me *The Message* by Eugene Peterson, a highly idiomatic translation of the Bible. I spent the three and a half hours of my flight reading through the book of Psalms. Whenever I came across a verse that captured the depth of the angst I was feeling or the sorrow I thought they might be feeling, I highlighted it. After I landed, I compiled those verses in a journal-type format. I simply put the verse at the top of a blank page and left lots of white space for them to respond to it and, subsequently, to God.

Over the years, I have revisited those verses. They have been helpful to me in my times of suffering because I don't always know what to pray. I don't know what is "in bounds" and what is "out of bounds" when it comes to giving vent to the depths of my sorrow. These verses often go much deeper than I would ever have dared. Some of the verses include words of hope. I don't always know how to find my own words for the hope I am seeking desperately. These verses give me assistance when my own words are silent.

I have included them in the following pages. There are fifty passages that stood out to me, although I know there are many, many more. You can use them as you like. Simply read the words of the verse(s) on the top of any page and let them penetrate your heart and mind. If they find resonance with what you are feeling, jot down some of your thoughts. In so doing, God will turn this book into a very personal work unique just to you. Don't feel obligated to follow any particular order as you go through the following pages; different verses will stand out to you at different times; and don't feel as though there is a time limit to "getting it done." You may spend months or years pondering the thoughts that God brings to your mind.

I pray that you come back to these pages over and over again. God is not afraid of our doubts or complaints. It is only through honest response that we discover what is truly going on in our hearts. May God use these verses to aid you in your heartfelt expressions during your times of grief. And may God meet you there.

The following Scriptures taken from The Message. Copyright ©
1993, 1994, 1995, 1996, 2000, 2001, 2002. Used by permission of
NavPress Publishing Group.

Psalm 3

² Hah! No help for him from God!"
³But you, GOD, shield me on all sides.

Yes!!

I will Not feel
over whelmed or afraid

for I know that My God
Walks with me!!

Psalm 4

⁸ For you, GOD, have put my life back together.

over and over again!
The way of life seems that
we never stay in comfortable
places for too long. They are only
rest stops along the way.
We rest, we go, we fall apart,
God restores and we rest once
again. We learn as we go.

Psalm 5

[1]Listen, GOD! Please, pay attention!
Can you make sense of these ramblings, [2]my groans and cries?
King-God, I need your help.
[3]Every morning you'll hear me at it again. Every morning I lay
out the pieces of my life on your altar and watch for fire to
descend.

Please do hear my crys
Father! I am hure and
angry and frustrated ...
only you can help me!
Come Lord Jesus, come!!

Psalm 6

⁶I'm tired of all this--so tired.
My bed has been floating forty days and nights
on the flood of my tears.
My mattress is soaked, soggy with tears.
⁷The sockets of my eyes are black holes;
nearly blind, I squint and grope.

Depression: so easy to fall
into; so difficult to climb
out of! Help me Lord!!

Psalm 10

[17]*The victim's faint pulse picks up; the hearts of the hopeless
pump red blood as you put your ear to their lips.*

?
Trusting + waiting?.
Don't quite get this one ----

Psalm 11

[1] I've already run for dear life straight to the arms of GOD, so why would I run away now?

Amen! You are all we have Lord There is no one or no thing other than you!! Help me snuggle down in your arms and wrap your cloak around me and let go of everything else but your presence, your love, your safety! Let me sit still!

Psalm 13

[1]*Long enough, GOD- you've ignored me long enough. I've looked at the back of your head long enough.* [2]*Long enough I've carried this ton of trouble, lived with a stomach full of pain. Long enough my arrogant enemies have looked down their noses at me.*

[5]*I've thrown myself headlong into your arms--*

and -- You catch me
and hold me
and give the answers
I have been searching
and longing for!
Thank you Jesus!

Psalm 16

2 Without you, nothing makes sense.

How absolutely true!!
There would be no reason to
continue on if there was
not you!

Psalm 17

⁵I'm staying on your trail.
I'm putting one foot in front of the other.
I'm not giving up.

I will hang on. I will trust in your love and grace Father.
I will
I will
I will . . . . . .

Psalm 18

[1]*I love you, GOD- you make me strong.* [2]*GOD is bedrock under*
my feet, the castle in which I live, my rescuing knight.
My God--the high crag where I run for dear life, hiding behind
the boulders, safe in the granite hideout.

I love this!! my rescuing
knight!-- awesome!!

why do we always look for
some human being to be
our "knight in shining armor"?--
when only Christ can be
that!

Psalm 20

[1]GOD answer you on the day you crash,

Oh - So many, many days!!
please don't just answer ---
Surround me in your cloak
of love and peace + joy!!

Psalm 22

[1]God, God . . . my God!
Why did you dump me miles from nowhere?
[2]Doubled up with pain, I call to God all the day long. No answer.
Nothing. I keep at it all night, tossing and turning.

Oh yes -- I know this!
I will keep calling!

Psalm 23

3True to your word, you let me catch my breath and send me in the right direction. 4Even when the way goes through Death Valley, I'm not afraid when you walk at my side. Your trusty shepherd's crook makes me feel secure.

Psalm 25

²²GOD, give your people a break from this run of bad luck.

Psalm 27

6 Already I'm singing God-songs;
I'm making music to GOD.

Psalm 30

[5] *The nights of crying your eyes out give way to days of laughter.*

Psalm 31

[9]Be kind to me, GOD-I'm in deep, deep trouble again. I've cried my eyes out; I feel hollow inside. [10]My life leaks away, groan by groan; my years fade out in sighs. My troubles have worn me out, turned my bones to powder.

[24]Be brave. Be strong. Don't give up.

Expect GOD to get here soon.

Psalm 32

⁶These things add up. Every one of us needs to pray; when all hell breaks loose and the dam bursts

Psalm 36

[5]God's love is meteoric
His loyalty astronomic
[6]His purpose titanic
His verdicts oceanic.

Yet in his largeness nothing gets lost;
Not a man, not a mouse, slips through the cracks.

Psalm 40

12 I was so swamped by guilt I couldn't see my way clear. More guilt in my heart than hair on my head, so heavy the guilt that my heart gave out.

Psalm 42

[1]A white-tailed deer drinks from the creek; I want to drink God, deep draughts of God. [2]I'm thirsty for God--alive.
I wonder, "Will I ever make it--arrive and drink in God's presence?" [3]I'm on a diet of tears--tears for breakfast, tears for supper.
[9]Sometimes I ask God, my rock-solid God, "Why did you let me down? Why am I walking around in tears?"

Psalm 55

[4]My insides are turned inside out; spectres of death have me down. [5]I shake with fear, I shudder from head to foot. [6]"Who will give me wings," I ask--"wings like a dove?" Get me out of here on dove wings

[7]I want some peace and quiet. I want a walk in the country, [8]I want a cabin in the woods. I'm desperate for a change from rage and stormy weather.

Psalm 57

²*I call out to High God, the God who holds me together.*

Psalm 61

^{1}God, listen to me shout, bend an ear to my prayer. ^{2}When I'm far from anywhere, down to my last gasp,

Psalm 65

¹Silence is praise to you, Zion--dwelling God, And also obedience.

²You hear the prayer in it all.

Psalm 68

*[19] Blessed be the Lord--day after day he carries us along. [20] He's
our Savior, our God, oh yes!
He's God--for--us
He's God--who-saves-us.
Lord GOD knows all death's ins and outs.*

Psalm 69

[3] I'm hoarse from calling for help, Bleary-eyed from searching the sky for God.

[29] I'm hurt and in pain; Give me space for healing, and mountain air.

Psalm 70

[5] But I've lost it. I'm wasted. God--quickly, quickly! Quick to my side, quick to my rescue!

GOD, don't lose a minute.

Psalm 72

⁴ Please help the children of the needy,
¹³He opens a place in his heart for the down--and-out, he restores the wretched of the earth. ¹⁴He frees them from tyranny and torture—

when they bleed, He bleeds; when they die, He dies.

Psalm 73

[11]What's going on here? Is God out to lunch? Nobody's tending the store.[12]The wicked get by with everything; they have it made, piling up riches

[13]I've been stupid to play by the rules; what has it gotten me?[14]A long run of bad luck, that's what--a slap in the face every time I walk out the door.[15] If I'd have given in and talked like this, I would have betrayed your dear children.[16] Still, when I tried to figure it out, all I got was a splitting headache . . .

[25] You're all I want in heaven! You're all I want on earth!

Psalm 75

[3] *When the earth goes topsy-turvy and nobody knows which end is up, I nail it all down, I put everything in place again.*

Psalm 77

[1] I yell out to my God, I yell with all my might, I yell at the top of my lungs.

He listens.

[2] I found myself in trouble and went looking for my Lord; my life was an open wound that wouldn't heal. When friends said, "Everything will turn out all right," I didn't believe a word they said. [3] I remember God--and shake my head. I bow my head--then wring my hands. [4] I'm awake all night--not a wink of sleep;

Psalm 80

[5]*You put us on a diet of tears, bucket after bucket of salty tears to drink.*

Psalm 81

⁵ *I hear this most gentle whisper from One I never guessed would speak to me:*

⁶ *"I took the world off your shoulders, freed you from a life of hard labour.* ⁷*You called to me in your pain; I got you out of a bad place."*

Psalm 88

¹ GOD, you're my last chance of the day. I spend the night on my knees before you.² Put me on your salvation agenda; take notes on the trouble I'm in.³ I've had my fill of trouble; I'm camped on the edge of hell.

Psalm 89

[49] So where is the love you're so famous for, Lord?

Psalm 90

¹² Oh! Teach us to live well! Teach us to live wisely and well!

¹³ Come back, GOD-how long do we have to wait?-
¹⁴Surprise us with love at daybreak;

Psalm 94

[17] If GOD hadn't been there for me, I never would have made it. [18] The minute I said, "I'm slipping, I'm falling," your love, GOD, took hold and held me fast. [19] When I was upset and beside myself, you calmed me down and cheered me up.

Psalm 103

⁶GOD makes everything come out right; He puts victims back on their feet.

¹³As parents feel for their children, GOD feels for those who fear Him

Psalm 109

²¹Oh, GOD, my Lord, step in; work a miracle for me--you can do it! Get me out of here--your love is so great!-
²²I'm at the end of my rope, my life in ruins.²³I'm fading away to nothing, passing away, my youth gone, old before my time.

²⁶Help me, oh help me, GOD, my God, save me through your wonderful love

Psalm 116

[16]Oh, GOD, here I am, your servant, your faithful servant: set me free for your service! [17]I'm ready to offer the thanksgiving sacrifice and pray in the name of GOD. [18]I'll complete what I promised GOD I'd do.

Psalm 119

[76]Oh, love me--and right now!-hold me tight! Just the way you promised. [77] Now comfort me so I can live, really live.

[98]Your commands give me an edge on my enemies; they never become obsolete.[99]I've even become smarter than my teachers since I've pondered and absorbed Your counsel.[100]I've become wiser than the wise old sages simply by doing what You tell me.

Psalm 121

[1]I look up to the mountains; does my strength come from mountains? [2]No, my strength comes from GOD, who made heaven, and earth, and mountains.

Psalm 125

[1]Those who trust in GOD are like Zion Mountain: Nothing can move it, a rock-solid mountain you can always depend on.[2]Mountains encircle Jerusalem, and GOD encircles his people--always has and always will.

Psalm 130

¹Help, GOD-the bottom has fallen out of my life! Master, hear my cry for help! ²Listen hard! Open your ears! Listen to my cries for mercy.

⁵I pray to GOD-my life a prayer--and wait for what He'll say and do. ⁶My life's on the line before God, my Lord

waiting and watching till morning

waiting and watching till morning.

Psalm 136

^{23}*God remembered us when we were down,*
His love never quits.

^{24}*Rescued us from the trampling boot,*
His love never quits.

^{25}*Takes care of everyone in time of need.*
His love never quits.

^{26}*Thank God, who did it all!*
His love never quits!

Psalm 139

¹⁶Like an open book, You watched me grow from conception to birth; all the stages of my life were spread out before You, the days of my life all prepared before I'd even lived one day.

Psalm 142

[4] *I'm up against it, with no exit--bereft, left alone.*[5]*I cry out, GOD, call out: "You're my last chance, my only hope for life!"* [6]*Oh listen, please listen; I've never been this low."*

Psalm 145

[18]GOD's there, listening for all who pray, for all who pray and mean it. [19]He does what's best for those who fear him--hears them call out, and saves them.

Psalm 147

³He heals the heartbroken and bandages their wounds.

ACKNOWLEDGEMENTS

As always, my first thanks go to my Heavenly Father for His incredible kindness and patience with me as I learn how to better live this life. He has been my confidence since my youth; I have relied on Him since birth. And He has never let me down.

I want to thank Jennifer for her constant love, friendship and encouragement. Thanks for believing in me and for your helpful comments on the earlier drafts.

I have had an extraordinary team of readers who have taken the time to think through what I have written and have given me helpful criticism. I could not have done this without you: Michael Bergmann, Bjorg Buhler, Kari Hauer, Amanda Strain, Ginny Wadge, Rick Thiessen, and Joel Roos.

I have been so lucky to have Heather Mueller involved in the process of editing all my books. Heather, you constantly make me appear much smarter than I am.

I am thankful for a few good friends who have stood by me throughout this entire ordeal of my suffering: Rod, Rick, Geoff, Jeremy, Amy, Brent, Brandon, Briana, Ron, and Lorne.

I am so grateful for my team of medical professionals and counselors who have journeyed with me through my illness and offered invaluable care and counsel: Rick Ward, Tavis Campbell, Melanie Driedger, Charles Coleman and Kevin McLaughlin.

I want to thank RockPointe Church (staff, elders and congregants) for all that they have had to endure as a result of my illness. You have treated me above and beyond what could ever have been expected.

Finally, I want to thank all those who have prayed tirelessly for Jennifer and I and the kids. I could never name you all as there are so many of you. I would not be at the place I am apart from your humble prayers to God on our behalf. Thank you, thank you, thank you!